DBQ Study Guide

Liberty, Equality, Power
A History of the American People
FIFTH EDITION

John M. Murrin
Princeton University, Emeritus

Paul E. Johnson
University of South Carolina, Emeritus

James M. McPherson
Princeton University, Emeritus

Alice Fahs
University of California, Irvine

Gary Gerstle
Vanderbilt University

Emily S. Rosenberg
University of California, Irvine

Norman L. Rosenberg
Macalester College

THOMSON
SOUTH-WESTERN

THOMSON
WADSWORTH

Australia · Brazil · Canada · Mexico · Singapore · Spain · United Kingdom · United States

DBQ Study Guide for AP US History
John M. Murrin, Paul E. Johnson, James M. McPherson, Alice Fahs,
Gary Gerstle, Emily S. Rosenberg, Norman L. Rosenberg

VP/Editorial Director:
Jack W. Calhoun, South-Western

VP/Editor-in-Chief:
P.J. Boardman, Wadsworth
Melissa Acuña South-Western

Acquisitions Editor:
Ashley Dodge, Wadsworth

Developmental Editor:
Margaret Beasley, Wadsworth

Marketing Manager:
Courtney Schulz, South-Western

Senior Content Project Manager:
Joshua Allen

Manufacturing Coordinator:
Charlene Taylor

**Development & Production
Service:**
Publishers Resource Group (PRG)

Printer:
West Publishing
Eagan, MN

Art Director:
Cate Rickard Barr

Cover Designer:
Cheryl Carrington

Cover Image:
"The Power of Music,"
William Sidney Mount
(1807–1868), courtesy
The Cleveland Museum of Art.
©Cleveland Museum of Art

For more information about our
products, contact us at:

Thomson Higher Education
5191 Natorp Boulevard
Mason, Ohio 45040
USA

A History of the American People

Activity Book

First European Contacts with Native Americans

Sources from *History Resource Center: U.S.*

Discovery of the New World, March 14, 1493

Source Citation: "Discovery of the New World, March 14, 1493." *DISCovering U.S. History*. Gale Research, 1997. Reproduced in History Resource Center. Farmington Hills, MI: Gale Group. http://galenet.galegroup.com/servlet/HistRC/ Document Number: BT2104210052

A letter written by Christopher Columbus (1451–1506) to one of his patrons, Lord Raphael Sanchez.

The Barcelona Letter

Source Citation: Columbus, Christopher. "The Barcelona Letter." Reproduced in History Resource Center. Farmington Hills, MI: Gale Group. http://galenet.galegroup.com/servlet/HistRC/ Document Number: CD2159000181

Writing to Luis de Santangel on February 15, 1493, Christopher Columbus (1451–1506) describes his arrival in what he believed to be the Indies. The description focuses on the region's inhabitants, vegetation, beauty, and potential wealth to Santangel, a treasurer of the court of Queen Isabel and King Ferdinand.

The Destruction of the Indies, 1542

Source Citation: "The Destruction of the Indies, 1542." *DISCovering U.S. History*. Gale Research, 1997. Reproduced in History Resource Center. Farmington Hills, MI: Gale Group. http://galenet.galegroup.com/servlet/HistRC/ Document Number: BT2104210070

As a Spanish missionary, Bartolomé de las Casas saw firsthand many of the cruel and destructive practices of the Spanish colonizers. This excerpt details some of the encounters between the indigenous people of America and the Spanish colonizers.

Excerpt from Description of Louisiana

Source Citation: Hennepin, Louis. "Excerpt from *Description of Louisiana*." Reproduced in History Resource Center. Farmington Hills, MI: Gale Group. http://galenet.galegroup.com/servlet/HistRC/ Document Number: CD2160000011

Father Louis Hennepin was the chaplain on French explorer René Robert La Salle's second expedition (1679–1680) that trekked through the upper Mississippi region. Early into the expedition, Hennepin was captured by the Sioux. Hennepin eventually returned to France where he published his travel narrative, *Description de la Louisiane*, complete with descriptions of what he saw in the Americas.

Letter of Jonas Michaelius

Source Citation: Michaelius, Jonas. "Letter of Jonas Michaelius." Reproduced in History Resource Center. Farmington Hills, MI: Gale Group.
http://galenet.galegroup.com/servlet/HistRC/
Document Number: CD2156000332

This letter from Jonas Michaelius, a minister from the Netherlands, was written on August 11, 1628, to his friend Adrian Smoutius, the founder of the first Dutch Reformed Church at New Amsterdam. Michaelius discusses his philosophy about educating and converting the indigenous people.

Excerpt from *A True Relation* (1608)

Source Citation: Smith, John. "Excerpt from *A True Relation* (1608)." Reproduced in History Resource Center. Farmington Hills, MI: Gale Group.
http://galenet.galegroup.com/servlet/HistRC/
Document Number: CD2161000099

A True Relation is the first history of the English settlement in the Chesapeake region written by Captain John Smith in 1608. In this excerpt Smith describes Native American women and their duties.

Memoir of Hernando de Escalante Fontaneda Respecting Florida of 1575

Source Citation: Escalante Fontaneda, Hernando de. "Memoir of Hernando de Escalante Fontaneda Respecting Florida of 1575." Reproduced in History Resource Center. Farmington Hills, MI: Gale Group.
http://galenet.galegroup.com/servlet/HistRC/
Document Number: CD2159000192

Born in Colombia of Spanish parents, Hernando de Escalante Fontaneda was sent to Spain at the age of thirteen to continue his education. On the journey across the Atlantic, Fontaneda was shipwrecked off the coast of Florida and was held captive by Native Americans for seventeen years. His memoir details his experiences.

Excerpt from The Relation

Source Citation: Cabeza de Vaca, Alvar Nuñez. "Excerpt from The Relation." Reproduced in History Resource Center. Farmington Hills, MI: Gale Group.
http://galenet.galegroup.com/servlet/HistRC/
Document Number: CD2159000321

Spanish explorer Alvar Nuñez Cabeza de Vaca traveled from present-day Texas throughout the Southwest. His encounters with Native Americans were sometimes friendly, his even being deemed a healer at times.

Excerpt from The Annals of the Cakchiquels

Source Citation: Unknown. "Excerpt from The Annals of the Cakchiquels." Reproduced in History Resource Center. Farmington Hills, MI: Gale Group.
http://galenet.galegroup.com/servlet/HistRC/
Document Number: CD2159000230

Written by an indigenous author, this document records the 1523 conquest of present-day Guatemala and El Salvador by Pedro de Alvarado (1485–1541).

The Prophecy and Advice of the Priest Xupan Nauat

Source Citation: Nauat, Xupan. "The Prophecy and Advice of the Priest Xupan Nauat." Reproduced in History Resource Center. Farmington Hills, MI: Gale Group. http://galenet.galegroup.com/servlet/HistRC/ Document Number: CD2159000223

This is a prophecy transcribed by a Mayan priest, Xupan Nauat, who warns of "the powerful white man" who will humiliate the Mayan warriors. A part of *The Books of the Chilam Balam*, this excerpt was written down by Mayan scribes.

Overview

Before 1492, the Western Hemisphere was populated with hundreds of cultures whose people spoke a multitude of languages. Indeed, there were roughly 250 tribes in North America at the time of Christopher Columbus's arrival. Many of these people belonged to societies with well-developed traditions of medicine, science, art, and religion. Furthermore, geographical isolation and ecological variety ensured that native cultures throughout this region would be extremely diverse.

Between 1492 and the 1690s, Europeans and Native Americans primarily encountered one another in four regions of North America: the East Coast (from the Arctic to the Carolinas); the Southeast (including the lower Mississippi Valley); the edge of Great Plains; and the Southwest. The heterogeneity of the indigenous peoples challenged European assumptions about the uniform and orderly nature of human origin.

A common European response to this cognitive dissonance was a tendency to become increasingly rigid in one's definitions of "human." Reports, letters, memoirs, and histories written by Europeans often note the "savage" and "strange" customs of the indigenous peoples. Although Captain John Smith describes the indigenous women as "very strong" and "able to endure to lie in the woods under a tree by the fire, in the worst of winter," he yet reports that they are "inconstant in everie thing [...] Some are of disposition fearefull, some bold, most cautelous, all Savage." Confronting the unexpected and unfamiliar, many early European explorers conflated the terms "different" and "savage."

Additionally, Eurocentric concepts of kinship, property, wealth, work, and gender were challenged by what explorers observed of the indigenous people. For example, Christopher Columbus and his crew encountered different concepts of property and the role that gifting plays in establishing relationship. Columbus describes how "They never refuse to give any thing away which is demanded of them, and will even themselves entreat an acceptance of their property" (Barcelona Letter). Furthermore, the oral and written traditions of the indigenous peoples suggest a similar grappling with

Courtesy of The Library of Congress, Washington, D.C.

Christopher Columbus Arriving at Hispaniola

Source Citation: Reproduced in History Resource Center. Farmington Hills, MI: Gale Group. http://galenet.galegroup.com/servlet/HistRC/ Document Number: CD2210014419

understanding who and what these visitors were. In an excerpt from *The Annals of the Cakchiquels*, an unnamed indigenous author records, "Thus did the Castilians enter of yore, O my children; but it was a fearful thing when they entered; their faces were strange, and the chiefs took them for gods." Undoubtedly the clash of worldviews contributed to problematic relations between the Europeans and the indigenous peoples.

From 1492, Native Americans began to die in large numbers, if not from war then from enslavement, mistreatment, despair, or disease. Accounts of the brutality the Native Americans suffered at the hands of the Europeans include reports by Spanish missionary Bartolomé de las Casas, who indicts the Spaniards who "do nothing save tear the natives to shreds, murder them and inflict upon them untold misery, suffering and distress, tormenting, harrying and persecuting them mercilessly." The records of the first encounters between Europeans and the Native Americans are not simple reports of easy contrasts; instead, the records reveal miscommunication and misunderstanding based on dissimilar perceptions of life and one's place in the world.

Activities

Focus Activity: Socratic Seminar

Socrates believed that disciplined conversation, based on the method of question and answer (dialectic), was the surest way to attain reliable knowledge. As historians who practice the process of critical inquiry, your task is to prepare a set of questions that evaluate, define, and clarify the underlying assumptions that the Europeans and the indigenous peoples brought with them into their first encounters. As a participant in the seminar, you help create a quality seminar when you listen actively, share your ideas and questions in response to others' ideas and questions, and use details from the primary sources to support your ideas.

Use the primary sources that follow to prepare your questions. For additional background information, search *History Resource Center: U.S.* using the keywords *conquerors*, *explorers*, or *discovery and exploration (America)*.

Discovery of the New World, March 14, 1493

The Barcelona Letter

The Destruction of the Indies, 1542

Excerpt from Description of Louisiana

Focus on Writing

Select one of these writing prompts to continue your investigation of "First European Contacts with Native Americans." Keep in mind the characteristics of the writing mode you choose. Also keep in mind the basic rules of grammar, usage, and mechanics.

Descriptive Writing: Compose a character sketch of Spanish missionary, Bartolomé de las Casas, based on details from his memoir. A character sketch highlights the important characteristics about a person using specific details to support each characteristic.

Expository Writing: Considering the accounts of contact between Europeans and Native Americans that you have read, write an essay that describes the difference between an "encounter" and a "conquest." Use information from the primary sources to explain and illustrate the differences.

Extension

Look through *History Resource Center: U.S.* to locate additional sources that relate to "First European Contacts with Native Americans." Think about the main topic of this lesson. Think about the sources already listed. This process will help you determine appropriate search words or phrases.

After you have compiled a list of sources, determine the best way to share your findings with your class. The types of sources you find may give you clues about the best method for sharing your findings.

Document-Based Essay Question (DBQ)

The following question requires you to construct a coherent essay that integrates your interpretation of Documents A–J and your knowledge of the period referred to in the question. Your essay should cite key pieces of evidence from the documents and draw on knowledge of Murrin, Chapter 1, "When Old Worlds Collide: Contact, Contrast, Catastrophe."

Both New England and the Chesapeake region of Virginia were primarily English settlements. What accounts for their subsequent development into two very different societies?

Use the documents and your knowledge of the period 1492–1690 to construct your essay.

Document A

Landing Negroes at Jamestown from Dutch Man-of-War, 1619

©Corbis

Source Citation: Reproduced in History Resource Center.
Farmington Hills, MI: Gale Group.
http://galenet.galegroup.com/servlet/HistRC/
Document Number: CD2210006805

The Mayflower Compact, November 11, 1620

In the Name of God, Amen. We, whose names are underwritten, the Loyal Subjects of our dread Sovereign Lord King James, by the Grace of God, of Great Britain, France, and Ireland, King, Defender of the Faith, &c. Having undertaken for the Glory of God, and Advancement of the Christian Faith, and the Honour of our King and Country, a Voyage to plant the first colony in the northern Parts of Virginia; Do by these Presents, solemnly and mutually in the Presence of God and one another, covenant and combine ourselves together into a civil Body Politick, for our better Ordering and Preservation, and Furtherance of the Ends aforesaid; And by Virtue hereof do enact, constitute, and frame, such just and equal Laws, Ordinances, Acts, Constitutions, and Offices, from time to time, as shall be thought most meet and convenient for the general Good of the Colony; unto which we promise all due Submission and Obedience. In WITNESS whereof we have hereunto subscribed our names at Cape Cod the eleventh of November, in the Reign of our Sovereign Lord King James of England, France, and Ireland, the eighteenth and of Scotland, the fifty-fourth. Anno Domini, 1620

Mr. John Carver	Mr. Samuel Fuller	Edward Tilly
Mr. William Bradford	Mr. Christopher Martin	John Tilly
Mr. Edward Winslow	Mr. William Mullins	Francis Cooke
Mr. William Brewster	Mr. William White	Thomas Rogers
Isaac Allerton	Mr. Richard Warren	Thomas Tinker
Miles Standish	John Howland	John Ridgate
John Alden	Mr. Stephen Hopkins	Edward Fuller
John Turner	Digery Priest	Richard Clark
Francis Eaton	Thomas Williams	Richard Gardiner
James Chilton	Gilbert Winslow	Mr. John Allerton
John Craxton	Edmund Margesson	Thomas English
John Billington	Peter Brown	Edward Doten
Joses Fletcher	Richard Bitteridge	Edward Liester
John Goodman	George Soule	

Source Citation: "The Mayflower Compact, November 11, 1620." *DISCovering U.S. History*. Gale Research, 1997. Reproduced in History Resource Center. Farmington Hills, MI: Gale Group. http://galenet.galegroup.com/servlet/HistRC/
Document Number: T2104210155

Graph of England's Colonial population, 1700

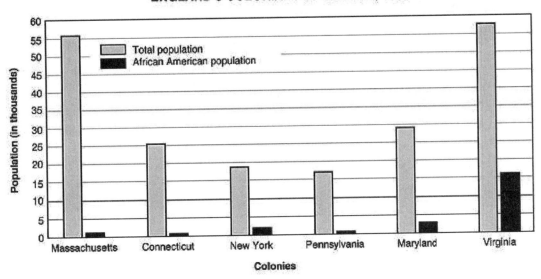

ENGLAND'S COLONIAL POPULATION, 1700

Source: Historical Statistics of the United States: Colonial Times to 1970.

Source Citation: Reproduced in History Resource Center. Farmington Hills, MI: Gale Group.
http://galenet.galegroup.com/servlet/HistRC/
Document Number: CD2210040968
(Illustration by George Barille. The Gale Group.)

A City Set Upon a Hill, 1651

And for ourselves here, the people of New England, we should in a special manner labor to shine forth in holiness above other people. We have that plenty and abundance of ordinances and means of grace, as few people enjoy the like; we are as a city set upon a hill, in the open view of all the earth, the eyes of the world are upon us, because we profess ourselves to be a people in covenant with God, and therefore not only the Lord our God, with whom we have made covenant, but heaven and earth, angels and men, that are witnesses of our profession, will cry shame upon us if we walk contrary to the covenant which we have professed and promised to walk in. If we open the mouths of men against our profession, by reason of the scandalousness of our lives, we (of all men) shall have the greater sin...

Let us study so to walk that this may be our excellency and dignity among the nations of the world among which we live; that they may be constrained to say of us, only this people is wise, a holy and blessed people; that all that see us may see and know that the name of the Lord is called upon us; and that we are the seed which the Lord hath blessed (Deut. 28:10; Isa. 61:9).

Source Citation: "A City Set Upon a Hill, 1651." *DISCovering U.S. History*. Gale Research, 1997. Reproduced in History Resource Center. Farmington Hills, MI: Gale Group.
http://galenet.galegroup.com/servlet/HistRC/
Document Number: BT2104210158

Document E

First English Settlers Landing at Roanoke Island

Anglorumin Virginiamaduentus. II.

Courtesy of The Library of Congress, Washington, D.C.

Source Citation: Reproduced in History Resource Center. Farmington Hills, MI: Gale Group.
http://galenet.galegroup.com/servlet/HistRC/
Document Number: CD2210015035

Document F

Excerpt from The Examination of Mrs. Ann Hutchinson at the court at Newtown

[…] Gov. Mrs. Hutchinson, the sentence of the court you hear is that you are banished from out of our jurisdiction as being a woman not fit for our society, and are to be imprisoned till the court shall send you away.

Mrs. H. I desire to know wherefore I am banished?

Gov. Say no more, the court knows wherefore and is satisfied.

Source Citation: Unknown. "The Examination of Mrs. Anne Hutchinson at the Court at Newtown." Reproduced in History Resource Center. Farmington Hills, MI: Gale Group.
http://galenet.galegroup.com/servlet/HistRC/
Document Number: CD2161000083

Document G

Excerpt from "Class" in *Violence in America*

[…] Bacon's Rebellion reveals overlapping contexts of class-related violence. This uprising, which engulfed the colony of Virginia in 1676, originated in a conflict between backcountry settlers and the Susquehannock Indians. Resentful over the lack of land available to freed servants and angered over the refusal of the colonial elite to commit troops to protect them from the Indians, the settlers, under the leadership of the well-born Nathaniel Bacon, Jr., launched an offensive against the colonial capital, drawing support from poor farmers, servants, craftsmen, and slaves along the way. Eventually, twenty-three of the rebels were executed (Bacon died of disease before he could be apprehended). What began as a battle between colonists and Indians had mushroomed into a challenge to elite authority. Within the coming years, colonial officials would seek to divert the attention of poor farmers from the injustices of colonial rule by bolstering the system of black slavery and awarding all white men regardless of status the right to bear arms and own land.[…]

Source Citation: "Class." *Violence in America*. Charles Scribner's Sons, 1999. Reproduced in History Resource Center. Farmington Hills, MI: Gale Group.
http://galenet.galegroup.com/servlet/HistRC/
Document Number: BT2350011067

The Trappan'd Maiden: Or, The Distressed Damsel (ballad)

> [...]
> Tune of Virginny, or, When that I was weary, weary, O.
>
> Give ear unto a Maid, that lately was betray'd,
> And sent into Virginny, O:
> In brief I shall declare, what I have suffer'd there,
> When that I was weary, weary, weary, weary, O.
>
> [Since] that first I came to this Land of Fame,
> Which is called Virginny, O,
> The Axe and the Hoe have wrought my overthrow,
> When that I was weary, weary, weary, weary, O.
>
> Five years served I, under Master Guy,
> In the land of Virginny, O,
> Which made me for to know sorrow, grief and woe,
> When that I was weary, weary, weary, weary, O.
>
> [...]
>
> So soon as it is day, to work I must away,
> In the Land of Virginny, O;
> Then my Dame she knocks, with her tinder-box,
> When that I am weary, weary, weary, weary, O.
>
> I have play'd my part both at Plow and Cart,
> In the Land of Virginny, O;
> Billets from the Wood upon my back they load,
> When that I am weary, weary, weary, weary, O.
>
> [...]

Source Citation: Unknown. "The Trappan'd Maiden Or, The Distressed Damsel." Reproduced in History Resource Center. Farmington Hills, MI: Gale Group.
http://galenet.galegroup.com/servlet/HistRC/
Document Number: CD2161000074

Document I

Letter from an English Immigrant to His Parents

Letter from Richard Frethorne to His Father and Mother

March 20, April 2 and 3, 1623

Manchester Papers, No. 325 Document in Public Record Office,
London List of Records No. 455

Loveing and kind father and mother my most humble duty remembred to you hopeing in God of yor good health, as I my selfe am at the makeing hereof, this is to let you vnderstand that I yor Child am in a most heavie Case by reason of the nature of the Country is such that it Causeth much sicknes, as the scurvie and the bloody flix, and divers other diseases, weh maketh the bodie very poore, and Weake, and when wee are sicke there is nothing to Comfort vs; for since I came out of the ship, I never at anie thing but pease, and loblollie (that is water gruell) [...] for wee are in great danger, for or Plantacon is very weake, by reason of the dearth, and sickness, of or Companie [Frethorne came to America as an employee of the Virginia Company of London], for wee came but Twentie for the marchaunte, and they are halfe dead Just; [...] ther is nothing to be gotten here but sicknes, and death [...]

Source Citation: Frethorne, Richard. "Letter from an English Immigrant to His Parents." Reproduced in History Resource Center. Farmington Hills, MI: Gale Group.
http://galenet.galegroup.com/servlet/HistRC/
Document Number: CD2154000007

Document J

Massachusetts Body of Liberties

Excerpts from The Massachusetts Body of Liberties (1641)

No man shall be beaten with above 40 stripes, nor shall any true gentleman, nor any man equall to a gentleman be punished with whipping, unles his crime be very shamefull, and his course of life vitious and profligate.

If any man at his death shall not leave his wife a competent portion of his estaite, upon just complaint made to the Generall Court she shall be relieved.

If any man after legall conviction shall have or worship any other god, but the lord god, he shall be put to death.

If any man or woeman be a witch, (that is hath or consulteth with a familiar spirit,) they shall be put to death.

Source Citation: Massachusetts Government. "Massachusetts Body of Liberties." Reproduced in History Resource Center. Farmington Hills, MI: Gale Group.
http://galenet.galegroup.com/servlet/HistRC/
Document Number: CD2163000002

The French and Indian War

Sources from *History Resource Center: U.S.*

A Letter from Quebeck to M. L'Maine a French Officer

Source Citation: [de La Roche]. A Letter from Quebeck to M. L'Maine a French Officer. Which Contains a Particular Account of the Present Designs of the French upon the English in North-America; what Force the French have Collected, their Several Divisions, and the Places Destin'd for Each. Likewise an Account of the Defenceless Condition of the English Provinces and Colonies, and the Methods made use of by the French, to Procure such Intelligence. Newport, Rhode-Island: Printed and Sold by J. Franklin, 1754. Reproduced in History Resource Center. Farmington Hills, MI: Gale Group. http://galenet.galegroup.com/servlet/HistRC/
Document Number: BT2700530001

A 1754 letter detailing the French plans for dealing with the English in North America.

Excerpt from A Memorial Concerning the Furr-Trade of the Province of New-York

Source Citation: Colden, Cadwallader. "Excerpt from A Memorial Concerning the Furr-Trade of the Province of New-York." Reproduced in History Resource Center. Farmington Hills, MI: Gale Group. http://galenet.galegroup.com/servlet/HistRC/
Document Number: CD2160000140

Cadwallader Colden, a physician and public servant, wrote about British prospects to overtake France in the North American fur trade. The 1724 letter describes the war to come.

The Expedition of Major General Braddock to Virginia

Source Citation: Unknown. The Expedition of Major General Braddock to Virginia; with the Two Regiments of Hacket and Dunbar. Being Extracts of Letters from an Officer in One of those Regiments to His Friend in London, Describing the March and Engagement in the Woods. Together with Many Little Incidents, Giving a Lively Idea of the Nature of the Country, Climate, and Manner in which the Officers and Soldiers Lived; Also the Difficulties they went through in that Wilderness. London: Printed for H. Carpenter, in Fleet-street, [1755]. Reproduced in History Resource Center. Farmington Hills, MI: Gale Group. http://galenet.galegroup.com/servlet/HistRC/
Document Number: BT2700950002

British Major General Edward Braddock was killed in 1754 in an attempt by the British to capture Fort Duquesne on the Ohio River. This account is by an unnamed British officer. (Suggested pages: 22–30)

The Christian Patriot

Source Citation: Maxwell, Hugh. "The Christian Patriot." Reproduced in History Resource Center. Farmington Hills, MI: Gale Group. http://galenet.galegroup.com/servlet/HistRC/
Document Number: CD2156000039

This biography of Hugh Maxwell was published by his daughter in 1833. Maxwell emigrated from Ireland to the colonies when he was six weeks old. He enlisted as a private during the French and Indian War and rose to the rank of colonel during the American Revolution.

The Second Journal of Christian Frederick Post

Source Citation: Post, Christian Frederick. The Second Journal of Christian Frederick Post, On a Message from the Governor of Pensilvania [sic] to the Indians on the Ohio. London: Printed for J. Wilkie, at the Bible and Sun, in St. Paul's Church-Yard, [1759]. Reproduced in History Resource Center. Farmington Hills, MI: Gale Group.
http://galenet.galegroup.com/servlet/HistRC/
Document Number: BT2700480001

As an emissary of the governor of Pennsylvania, Christian Post records his travels at the time of the French and Indian War. Reports of discussions with different Native American leaders indicate their concerns of losing land to the British and attempts to secure their allegiance. (Suggested pages: 11–16)

Recollections of an Old Soldier

Source Citation: Perry, David. Recollections of an Old Soldier. The Life of Captain David Perry, a Soldier of the French and Revolutionary Wars. Containing Many Extraordinary Occurrences Relating to His Own Private History, and an Account of Some Interesting Events in the History of the Times in which He Lived, No-Where Else Recorded, Windsor, VT. Printed and for sale at the Republican and Yeoman Printing Office, 1822. Reproduced in History Resource Center. Farmington Hills, MI: Gale Group.
http://galenet.galegroup.com/servlet/HistRC/
Document Number: BT2700630001

This memoir of Captain David Perry offers a British colonist's perspective on the events of the French and Indian War in the Lake George region. (Suggested pages: 6–12)

Memoirs of Major Robert Stobo

Source Citation: Stobo, Robert. *Memoirs of Major Robert Stobo, of the Virginia Regiment*. Pittsburgh: Published by John S. Davidson, No. 65 Market Street. Printed at the Office of Kennedy's Bank Note Review, Third St., 1854. Reproduced in History Resource Center. Farmington Hills, MI: Gale Group.
http://galenet.galegroup.com/servlet/HistRC/
Document Number: BT2700740003

Major Robert Stobo, of the Virginia Regiment, was captured as a British spy who shared plans to take Fort Duquesne, Pennsylvania. (Suggested pages: 17–21)

Albany Plan of Union

Source Citation: Franklin, Benjamin. "Albany Plan of Union." Reproduced in History Resource Center. Farmington Hills, MI: Gale Group.
http://galenet.galegroup.com/servlet/HistRC/
Document Number: CD2153000023

This document is Benjamin Franklin's 1754 plan for the colonies to form a self-governing federation under the British Crown.

Proclamation of 1763

Source Citation: "Proclamation of 1763, October 7, 1763." *DISCovering U.S. History*. Gale Research, 1997. Reproduced in History Resource Center. Farmington Hills, MI: Gale Group.
http://galenet.galegroup.com/servlet/HistRC/
Document Number: BT2104241056

On the heels of victory in the French and Indian War, King George III issued a proclamation forbidding European settlement beyond the Appalachian Mountains in an attempt to maintain control over the colonists and the Native Americans.

Louis XV's Proclamation on the Origins of the Seven Years' War

Source Citation: "Louis XV's Proclamation on the Origins of the Seven Years' War." *DISCovering World History*. Gale Research, 1997. Reproduced in History Resource Center. Farmington Hills, MI: Gale Group. http://galenet.galegroup.com/servlet/HistRC/
Document Number: BT2105210054

Louis XV justifies his recent alliance with Austria in response to Great Britian and Prussia's actions contesting trade and the colonies that caused, in his eyes, the Seven Years' War.

Overview

As France and Great Britain both worked toward building separate empires in North America, they engaged in a series of four colonial wars. The French and Indian War (1754–1763), the fourth, was part of this competition for land, resources, wealth, and dominance and the only war to begin in North America.

The French and Indian War began as a territorial dispute over the Ohio Valley among the French, the British, and the Iroquois Confederacy. Although the French claimed the region around the Great Lakes, it was the Iroquois Confederacy (also known as the Six Nations) who had controlled the region since the mid-seventeenth century. However, by the 1740s, British traders began making inroads into the area, which tested the Confederacy's stance of neutrality. In 1753, George Washington was sent by the Ohio Company (a group of Virginia land speculators) to demand that the French evacuate Fort LeBoeuf, which the British claimed was built on Virginia territory. The French refused, and Washington, along with 150 men, tried to force the French out, initiating the armed conflict.

The French and Indian War highlighted the effectiveness of different battle strategies. From the British perspective, the French and Indians were uncivilized in their use of guerilla tactics. Captain David Perry, a British colonist, reports, "In the year 1757, Gen. Mont Calm came against Fort George, with a large army of French and Indians, and obliged the garrison to surrender; after which, contrary to his express agreement, he let loose his Indians upon our men, and massacred a great many of them."

The French and Indian War resulted in the loss of France's North American empire and caused a significant shift in the relationship between Great Britain and its colonies as the British Parliament decided to pay for the war debt by raising taxes in the colonies.

Activities

Focus Activity: Four Corners Debate

You will debate the causes and effects of the French and Indian War from one of four perspectives: the French, the Iroquois, the British, or the colonists (wild card). Each corner will have time to discuss the assigned readings, and time to prepare a list of three causes and three effects of the French and Indian War from one perspective. You will need to appoint a spokesperson who can articulate your group's reasoning behind your stated causes and effects. Each spokesperson will have two minutes to present each group's cause and effect perspective. Next, each group will have one minute to rebut other groups' claims.

Use the primary sources that follow to prepare your group's position and reasoning. For additional background information, search *History Resource Center: U.S.* using the keywords *Seven Years War* or *Peace of Paris*.

A Letter from Quebeck to M. L'Maine a French Officer

Excerpt from A Memorial Concerning the Furr-Trade of the Province of New-York

The Expedition of Major General Braddock to Virginia

The Christian Patriot

The Second Journal of Christian Frederick Post

Recollections of an Old Soldier

Memoirs of Major Robert Stobo

Albany Plan of Union

Proclamation of 1763

Louis XV's Proclamation on the Origins of the Seven Years' War

Focus On Writing

Select one of these writing prompts to continue your investigation of the French and Indian War. Keep in mind the characteristics of the writing mode you choose. Also keep in mind the basic rules of grammar, usage, and mechanics.

Narrative Writing: Write a short story about a fictional fur trader during the French and Indian War. Include details and events from the primary sources to make the story realistic. Tell about your character's fears and hopes for the outcome of the fighting.

Persuasive Writing: Many of the British soldiers fighting in the French and Indian War accused the French and the Native Americans of brutal and uncivilized tactics. Considering the details from the primary sources, particularly any descriptions of battle, is there a "civilized" way of fighting? Write an essay on this issue. Support your answer with good reasons.

Extension

Look through *History Resource Center: U.S.* to locate additional sources that relate to the French and Indian War. Think about the main topic of this lesson. Think about the sources already listed. This process will help you determine appropriate search words or phrases.

After you have compiled a list of sources, determine the best way to share your findings with your class. The types of sources you find may give you clues about the best method for sharing your findings.

Document-Based Essay Question (DBQ)

The following question requires you to construct a coherent essay that integrates your interpretation of Documents A–I and your knowledge of the period referred to in the question. Your essay should cite key pieces of evidence from the documents and draw on knowledge of Murrin, Chapter 4, "Provincial America and the Struggle for a Continent."

The Great Awakening is often characterized as a counter-response to Enlightenment ideas; yet, both were part of a greater transatlantic exchange of ideas. To what extent did these two major movements of the eighteenth century help the people of the American colonies become more like each other than like Englishmen?

Use the documents and your knowledge of the period 1690–1790 to construct your essay.

Excerpt of Common Sense

In short, independence is the only bond that can tie and keep us together. We shall then see our object, and our ears will be legally shut against the schemes of an intriguing, as well as a cruel enemy. We shall then too be on a proper footing to treat with Britain; for there is reason to conclude, that the pride of that court will be less hurt by treating with the American states for terms of peace, than with those she denominates "rebellious subjects," for terms of accommodation. It is our delaying it that encourages her to hope for conquest, and our backwardness tends only to prolong the war. As we have, without any good effect therefrom, withheld our trade to obtain a redress of our grievances, let us now try the alternative, by independently redressing them ourselves, and then offering to open the trade. The mercantile and reasonable part in England will be still with us; because, peace with trade, is preferable to war without it.

Source Citation: "Excerpt of Common Sense." *American Journey Online: The American Revolution.* Primary Source Microfilm, 1999. Reproduced in History Resource Center. Farmington Hills, MI: Gale Group.
http://galenet.galegroup.com/servlet/HistRC/
Document Number: CD2153000077

Document B

**Excerpt from "'I saw the book talk': slave readings of the first great awakening."
Lambert, Frank.**

For most eighteenth-century slave converts, worship meant settings controlled by their white
masters. Charles Woodmason, an Anglican itinerant, noted the unusual degree of racial
intermixture in churches of the Carolina backcountry in the 1760s. Of a congregation at
Flatt Creek, Woodmason remarked: "Here I found a vast Body of People assembled -- Such
a Medley! such a mixed Multitude of all Classes and Complexions I never saw."(49) To the
Methodist circuit rider Thomas Rankin, the sight of blacks and whites in the same church was
commonplace. He observed in the 1770s that "hundreds of negroes" crowded in and around
Piedmont Virginia's evangelical chapels; "in general, the white people were within the chapel
and the black people without."

The Journal of Negro History, Fall 1992 v77 n4 p185(14)
Article A14321279
Association for the Study of African American Life, permission pending

Document C

**Editorial in *The Independent Reflector*, by the New York "Triumvirate,"
William Livingston, John Morin Scott, and William Smith (1753)**

A Printer ought not to publish every Thing that is offered to him; but what is conducive of
general Utility, he should not refuse, be the Author a Christian, Jew, Turk or Infidel. Such
Refusal is an immediate abridgement of the Freedom of the Press. When on the other Hand,
he prostitutes his Art by the Publication of any Thing injurious to his Country, it is criminal....
It is high Treason against the State. The usual Alarm rung in such Cases, the common Cry of
an Attack upon the LIBERTY OF THE PRESS, is groundless and trifling. The Press neither
has, nor can have such a Liberty, and whenever it is assumed, the Printer should be punished.

Source Citation: Levy, Leonard W. "Free Press in Colonial America." Reproduced in History Resource Center. Farmington
Hills, MI: Gale Group.
http://galenet.galegroup.com/servlet/HistRC/
Document Number: CD2163000033

**A Narrative of the Lord's Wonderful Dealings with John Marrant,
a Black, (Now Going to Preach the Gospel in Nova-Scotia)
Born in New-York, in North-America**

I John Marrant, born June 15th, 1755, in New-York, in North-America, with these gracious dealings of the Lord with me to be published, in hopes they may be useful to others, to encourage the fearful, to confirm the wavering, and to refresh the hearts of true believers. [...] So we went, and with much difficulty got within the doors. I was pushing the people to make room, to get the horn off my shoulder to blow it, just as Mr Whitefield was naming his text, and looking round, as I thought, directly upon me, and pointing with his finger, he uttered these words, "Prepare to meet thy God O Israel." The Lord accompanied the word with such power, that I was struck to the ground, and lay both speechless and senseless near half an hour. [...] When the people were dismissed Mr. Whitefield came into the vestry, and being told of my condition he came immediately, and the first word he said to me was, "Jesus Christ has got thee at last." [...] I used to spend my time in reading God's Word, singing Watts's Hymns and in Prayer, the little negro children would often come round the door with their pretty wishful looks, and finding my heart much drawn out in Love to their souls, I one evening called several of them in, and asked them if they could say the Lord's Prayer, &c. finding they were very ignorant, I told them, if they would come every evening I would teach them, which they did, and learned very fast, some of them in about four weeks could say the Lord's Prayer, and good part of the Catechism, after teaching, I used to go to prayer with them before we parted; this continued without interruption for three or four months, in which time, by the children acquainting their parents with it, I soon had my society increased to about thirty persons;

Document E

Preamble to the *Declaration of Independence* (1776)

When in the Course of human events, it becomes necessary for one people to dissolve the political bands which have connected them with another, and to assume among the Powers of the earth, the separate and equal station to which the Laws of Nature and of Nature's God entitle them, a decent respect to the opinions of mankind requires that they should declare the causes which impel them to the separation.

Source Citation: "Text of the Declaration of Independence, July 4, 1776." *DISCovering U.S. History*. Gale Research, 1997. Reproduced in History Resource Center. Farmington Hills, MI: Gale Group.
http://galenet.galegroup.com/servlet/HistRC/
Document Number: CD2104210078

Document F

Black Poet's Letter on Liberty, February 11, 1774

Revered and honoured Sir,

"I have this day received your obliging kind epistle, and am greatly satisfied with your reasons respecting the negroes, and think highly reasonable what you offer in vindication of their natural rights: Those that invade them cannot be insensible that the divine light is chasing away the thick darkness which broods over the land of Africa; and the chaos which has reigned so long, is converting into beautiful order, and reveals more and more clearly the glorious dispensation of civil and religious liberty, which are so inseparably united, that there is little or no enjoyment of one without the other; Otherwise, perhaps, the Israelites had been less solicitous for their freedom from Egyptian slavery; I do not say they would have been contented without it, by no means; for in every human breast God has implanted a principle, which we call love of freedom; it is impatient of oppression, and pants for deliverance; and by the leave of our modern Egyptians I will assert, that the same principle lives in us. God grant deliverance in his own way and time, and get him honour upon all those whose avarice impels them to countenance and help forward the calamities of their fellow creatures. This I desire not for their hurt, but to convince them of the strange absurdity of their conduct, whose words and actions are so diametrically opposite. How well the cry for liberty, and the reverse disposition for the exercise of oppressive power over others agree--I humbly think it does not require the penetration of a philosopher to determine."

Source Citation: Wheatley, Phillis. "Black Poet's Letter on Liberty, Feb. 11, 1774." Reproduced in History Resource Center. Farmington Hills, MI: Gale Group.
http://galenet.galegroup.com/servlet/HistRC/
Document Number: CD2153000199

Document G

Maxims from Poor Richard's Almanack, by Benjamin Franklin

Dost thou love life? Then do not squander time; for that's the stuff life is made of.

Great talkers, little doers.

God helps them that help themselves.

In the affairs of this world, men are saved not by faith but by the want of it.

Source Citation: Franklin, Benjamin. "Maxims from Poor Richard's Almanack." Reproduced in History Resource Center. Farmington Hills, MI: Gale Group.
http://galenet.galegroup.com/servlet/HistRC/
Document Number: CD2153000200

Document H

Philip Freneau "The Rising Glory of America" (1771)

[...] This is the land of every joyous sound,/

Of liberty and life, sweet liberty!/

Without whose aid the noblest genius/

fails,/

And science irretrievably must die.

Source Citation: "The Enlightenment." *Encyclopedia of the North American Colonies.* 3 vols. Charles Scribner's Sons, 1993. Reproduced in History Resource Center. Farmington Hills, MI: Gale Group.
http://galenet.galegroup.com/servlet/HistRC/
Document Number: BT2350023092

A Primer for the Use of the Mohawk Children

©Bettman/Corbis

The Cotton South in Antebellum America

Sources from *History Resource Center: U.S.*

Plantation Life as Viewed by Ex-Slave

Source Citation: Kinney, Nicey (as told to Grace McCune). "Plantation Life as Viewed by Ex-Slave."
Reproduced in History Resource Center. Farmington Hills, MI: Gale Group.
http://galenet.galegroup.com/servlet/HistRC/
Document Number: CD2161000057

This is an 1838 interview of a former slave.

The Freedman's Story

Source Citation: Parker, William. "The Freedman's Story." Reproduced in History Resource Center.
Farmington Hills, MI: Gale Group.
http://galenet.galegroup.com/servlet/HistRC/
Document Number: CD2152000628

This is a memoir by a slave who escaped to freedom.

The Narrative of Lewis Clarke

Source Citation: Clarke, Lewis. "The Narrative of Lewis Clarke." Reproduced in History Resource Center.
Farmington Hills, MI: Gale Group.
http://galenet.galegroup.com/servlet/HistRC/
Document Number: CD2152000029

This is a memoir by the son of an Irish immigrant and slave woman who lived as a slave for twenty years
before escaping to the North.

Excerpt from *Darkness Cometh the Light, or, Struggles for Freedom*

Source Citation: Delaney, Lucy A. "Excerpt from *Darkness Cometh the Light; or, Struggles for Freedom*."
Reproduced in History Resource Center. Farmington Hills, MI: Gale Group.
http://galenet.galegroup.com/servlet/HistRC/
Document Number: CD2161000056

In this book a woman recounts her years as a slave, a fugitive slave, and a free woman.

A North-Side View of Slavery

Source Citation: Little, John (Mrs.). "A North-Side View of Slavery." Reproduced in History Resource
Center. Farmington Hills, MI: Gale Group.
http://galenet.galegroup.com/servlet/HistRC/
Document Number: CD2152000568

This is a memoir by a fugitive slave in Canada, probably in the 1850s, of her life in slavery and the accounts of her and her husband's escape.

Draft of a Bill Concerning Slaves, Free Negroes and Mulattoes

Source Citation: "Draft of a Bill Concerning Slaves, Free Negroes and Mulattoes." Reproduced in History Resource Center. Farmington Hills, MI: Gale Group.
http://galenet.galegroup.com/servlet/HistRC/
Document Number: CD2152000192

This is legislation by the Virginia House of Delegates after the insurrection led by Nat Turner (1831), which reduced the rights of free blacks and mulattoes.

Excerpt from *My Bondage and My Freedom*

Source Citation: Douglass, Frederick. "Excerpt from *My Bondage and My Freedom*." Reproduced in History Resource Center. Farmington Hills, MI: Gale Group.
http://galenet.galegroup.com/servlet/HistRC/
Document Number: CD2152000600

This is an excerpt of a memoir by Frederick Douglass telling of his early life with his grandparents and his separation from them.

On the Underground Railroad, c. 1850

Source Citation: "On the Underground Railroad, c. 1850." *DISCovering U.S. History*. Gale Research, 1997. Reproduced in History Resource Center. Farmington Hills, MI: Gale Group.
http://galenet.galegroup.com/servlet/HistRC/
Document Number: BT2104210112

This is a memoir by a Quaker who was reported to be the president of the Underground Railroad.

Excerpt from *The Fugitive Blacksmith*

Source Citation: Pennington, James W.C. "Excerpt from *The Fugitive Blacksmith*." Reproduced in History Resource Center. Farmington Hills, MI: Gale Group.
http://galenet.galegroup.com/servlet/HistRC/
Document Number: CD2152000574

This book, published in 1849, tells a fugitive slave's narrative by a man who became a minister and an abolitionist.

Excerpt from *Bible Defense of Slavery: 1*

Source Citation: Anonymous. "Excerpt from *Bible Defense of Slavery: 1*." Reproduced in History Resource Center. Farmington Hills, MI: Gale Group.
http://galenet.galegroup.com/servlet/HistRC/
Document Number: CD2152000043

This is an anonymous defense of slavery published in a tract titled *Bible Defense of Slavery* by Josiah Priest.

Excerpt from *Bible Defense of Slavery: 2*

Source Citation: Campbell, A. (Rev.). "Excerpt from *Bible Defense of Slavery: 2*." Reproduced in History Resource Center. Farmington Hills, MI: Gale Group.
http://galenet.galegroup.com/servlet/HistRC/
Document Number: CD2152000044

This is a sermon by Rev. A. Campbell published in *Bible Defense of Slavery* by Josiah Priest.

The Rights and the Duties of Masters

Source Citation: Thornwell, J[ames] H[enley], Rev. The Rights and the Duties of Masters. *A Sermon Preached at the Dedication of a Church, Erected in Charleston, S.C., for the Benefit and Instruction of the Coloured Population.* Charleston, S.C. Steam Power Press of Walker & James, 1850. Reproduced in History Resource Center. Farmington Hills, MI: Gale Group.
http://galenet.galegroup.com/servlet/HistRC/
Document Number: BT2705230001

This is a sermon defending slavery.

Overview

After 1815, the southern economy became dependent on cotton as its main cash crop, and the need for slaves increased significantly. From then until the Civil War (1861–1865), cotton and slavery were linked in the South.

From 1820 to 1860, the worldwide demand for cotton increased yearly. Production rose from 150,000 bales in 1812 to 3.8 million bales in 1860. The number of African Americans enslaved in the South rose from 690,000 in 1790 to two million in 1830 and to four million in 1850. Importation of slaves was outlawed in the United States in 1808, so most of the slave population after that time was native-born. Slaveholding families, however, made up only a small percentage of the southern population. By 1860, only 12 percent of white southerners owned 20 or more slaves, and only 1 percent owned 100 or more slaves. Even though their numbers were small, southern slaveholders wielded the power in the South.

Slaves and their children were the property of their masters. They could be sold and families split. Life was hard for slaves, most of whom worked in fields from sunup to sunset. As a rule, slaves lacked adequate housing, clothing, and food. Owners relied on a system of rewards and punishments to maintain control over their slaves. Another attempt to maintain control made it illegal to teach slaves to read and write. Slaves, however, often found ways to "manage" the workload by methods such as losing livestock, damaging equipment, and faking ignorance and superstition.

Slave Auction at Richmond, Virginia

Source Citation: Reproduced in History Resource Center. Farmington Hills, MI: Gale Group.
http://galenet.galegroup.com/servlet/HistRC/
Document Number: CD2210006797

Although most slaves found it best to find ways to work within the system, some did attempt to escape. Slaves in the upper South were more successful in escaping to the North because of the shorter distance. Many slaves successfully used the Underground Railroad, a system whereby blacks and whites smuggled slaves along predetermined routes to the North.

By 1860, the system of slavery was so entrenched in the Southern economy and culture that defending it became necessary. Slavery ended in the United States when the North won the Civil War and freed the slaves.

Activities

Focus Activity: Slave Dialogues

You are a fugitive slave in antebellum America. You are exchanging stories with a slave you met on the Underground Railroad, telling of your life as a slave and your escape. Prepare a five-minute dialogue with your partner to illustrate different situations in which slaves lived.

Use the primary sources that follow to prepare your dialogue. For additional information, search *History Resource Center: U.S.* using the keyword *slaves, slavery, plantation life,* and *Underground Railroad.*

The Narrative of Lewis Clarke

The Freedman's Story

On the Underground Railroad, c. 1850

The Fugitive Blacksmith

Focus on Writing

Select one of these writing prompts to continue your investigation of southern slaves in antebellum America. Keep in mind the characteristics of the writing mode you choose. Also keep in mind the basic rules of grammar, usage, and mechanics.

Descriptive Writing: Using everyday English, write a poem describing slavery in the South during antebellum times. Use information from the primary sources and from your background reading to make the poem realistic.

Expository Writing: You are a northern journalist traveling through the South in the 1850s. Write a magazine article denouncing slavery. Use information from the primary sources and from your background reading to support your position.

Extension

Look through *History Resource Center: U.S.* to locate additional sources that relate to slaves in antebellum America. Think about the main topic of this lesson. Think about the sources already listed. This process will help you determine appropriate search words or phrases.

After you have compiled a list of sources, determine the best way to share your findings with your class. The types of sources you find may give you clues about the best method for sharing your findings.

Document-Based Essay Question (DBQ)

The following questions require you to construct a coherent essay that integrates your interpretation of Documents A–G and your knowledge of the period referred to in the questions. Your essay should cite key pieces of evidence from the documents and draw on knowledge of Murrin, Chapter 10, "Toward an American Culture" and Chapter 11, "Society, Culture, and Politics, 1820s–1840s."

Analyze slave life in the South during antebellum times. What were some of the conditions of slave life as described by fugitive and/or former slaves? What were some of the defenses of slavery used during that time? What were some methods of escape used by slaves?

Use the documents and your knowledge of the period from 1820 through 1861 to construct your essay.

Document A

A North-Side View of Slavery

Excerpt from the Refugee: Or the Narratives of Fugitive Slaves in Canada, by Benjamin Drew

Mrs. John Little.

I was born in Petersburg, Va. When very young, I was taken to Montgomery county. My old master died there, and I remember that all the people were sold. My father and mother were sold together about one mile from me. After a year, they were sold a great distance, and I saw them no more. My mother came to me before she went away, and said, "Good by, be a good girl; I never expect to see you any more."

Then I belonged to Mr. T----- N-----, the son of my old master. He was pretty good, but his wife, my mistress, beat me like sixty. Here are three scars on my right hand and arm, and one on my forehead, all from wounds inflicted with a broken china plate. My cousin, a man, broke the plate in two pieces, and she said, "Let me see that plate." I handed up the pieces to her, and she threw them down on me: they cut four gashes, and I bled like a butcher.

Source Citation: Little, John (Mrs.). "A North-Side View of Slavery." Reproduced in History Resource Center. Farmington Hills, MI: Gale Group. http://galenet.galegroup.com/servlet/HistRC/ Document Number: CD2152000568

Plantation Life as Viewed by Ex-Slave

Plantation Life as Viewed by Ex-Slave, Nicey Kinney, as told to Miss Grace McCune

A narrow path under large water oaks led through a well-kept yard where a profusion of summer flowers surrounded Nicey Kinney's two-story frame house. The porch floor and a large portion of the roof had rotted down, and even the old stone chimney at one end of the structure seemed to sag. The middle-aged mulatto woman who answered the door shook her head when asked if she was Nicey Kinney. "No, mam," she protested, "but dat's my mother and she's sick in bed. She gits mighty lonesome lyin' dar in de bed and she sho does love to talk. Us would be mighty proud if you would come in and see her."

Nicey was propped up in bed and, although the heat of the September day was oppressive, the sick woman wore a black shoulder cape over her thick flannel nightgown; heavy quilts and blankets were piled close about her thin form, and the window at the side of her bed was tightly closed. Not a lock of her hair escaped the nightcap that enveloped her head. The daughter removed an empty food tray and announced, "Mammy, dis lady's come to see you and I 'spects you is gwine to lax her fine 'cause she wants to hear 'bout dem old days dat you loves so good to tell about." Nicey smiled. "I'se so glad you come to see me," she said, "'cause I gits so lonesome; jus' got to stay here in dis bed, day in and day out. I'se done wore out wid all de hard wuk I'se had to do, and now I'se a aged 'oman, done played out and sufferin' wid de high blood pressur'. But I kin talk and I does love to bring back dem good old days a-fore de war."

Source Citation: Kinney, Nicey (as told to Grace McCune). "Plantation Life as Viewed by Ex-Slave." Reproduced in History Resource Center. Farmington Hills, MI: Gale Group.
http://galenet.galegroup.com/servlet/HistRC/
Document Number: CD2161000057

The Freedman's Story

Early Plantation Life.

I was born opposite to Queen Anne, in Anne Arundel County, in the State of Maryland, on a plantation called Rowdown. My master was Major William Brogdon, one of the wealthy men of that region. He had two sons, -- William, a doctor, and David, who held some office at Annapolis, and for some years was a member of the Legislature.

Like every Southern plantation of respectable extent and pretensions, our place had what is called the "Quarter," or place where the slaves of both sexes are lodged and fed. With us the Quarter was composed of a number of low buildings, with an additional building for single people and such of the children as were either orphans or had parents sold away or otherwise disposed of. This building was a hundred feet long by thirty wide, and had a large fireplace at either end, and small rooms arranged along the sides. In these rooms the children were huddled from day to day, the smaller and weaker subject to the whims and caprices of the larger and stronger. The largest children would always seize upon the warmest and best places, and say to us who were smaller, "Stand back, little chap, out of my way"; and we had to stand back or get a thrashing.

Source Citation: Parker, William. "The Freedman's Story." Reproduced in History Resource Center. Farmington Hills, MI: Gale Group.
http://galenet.galegroup.com/servlet/HistRC/
Document Number: CD2152000628

The Narrative of Lewis Clarke

Excerpt from The Narrative of Lewis Clarke

There were about one hundred and fifteen slaves upon this plantation. Generally, we have enough, in quantity, of food. We had, however, but two meals a day, of corn-meal bread and soup, or meat of the poorest kind. Very often, so little care had been taken to cure and preserve the bacon, that, when it came to us, though it had been fairly killed once, it was more alive than dead. Occasionally, we had some refreshment over and above the two meals, but this was extra, beyond the rules of the plantation. And, to balance this gratuity, we were also frequently deprived of our food, as a punishment. We suffered greatly, too, for want of water. The slave-drivers have the notion that slaves are more healthy, if allowed to drink but little, than they are if freely allowed nature's beverage. The slaves quite as confidently cherish the opinion that, if the master would drink less peach brandy and whisky, and give the slave more water, it would be better all around. As it is, the more the master and overseer drink, the less they seem to think the slave needs.

Source Citation: Clarke, Lewis. "The Narrative of Lewis Clarke." Reproduced in History Resource Center. Farmington Hills, MI: Gale Group.
http://galenet.galegroup.com/servlet/HistRC/
Document Number: CD2152000029

On the Underground Railroad, c. 1850

Levi Coffin, a Quaker, was the reputed "president" of the Underground Railroad.

The fugitives generally arrived in the night, and were secreted among the friendly colored people or hidden in the upper room of our house. They came alone or in companies, and in a few instances had a white guide to direct them.

One company of twenty-eight that crossed the Ohio River at Lawrenceburg, Indiana--twenty miles below Cincinnati--had for conductor a white man whom they had employed to assist them. The character of this man was full of contradictions. He was a Virginian by birth and spent much of his time in the South, yet he hated slavery. He was devoid of moral principle, but was a true friend to the poor slave. ...

... The company of twenty-eight slaves referred to, all lived in the same neighborhood in Kentucky, and had been planning for some time how they could make their escape from slavery. This white man--John Fairfield--had been in the neighborhood for some weeks buying poultry, etc., for market, and though among the whites he assumed to be very pro-slavery, the negroes soon found that he was their friend.

Source Citation: "On the Underground Railroad, c. 1850." *DISCovering U.S. History.* Gale Research, 1997. Reproduced in History Resource Center. Farmington Hills, MI: Gale Group.
http://galenet.galegroup.com/servlet/HistRC/
Document Number: BT2104210112

Excerpt from *Bible Defense of Slavery: 1*

Excerpt from Bible Defense of Slavery, by Josiah Priest

But we are told that slavery is an evil. So is war an evil. And, viewing it in the same light, government may also be considered an evil, since it is an abridgement of liberty. Yet have they both received the sanction, and continue to exist, by the appointment of an all-wise and beneficent Providence. There is, probably, not a succession of seasons, of day and night, of sunshine and storm, which we cannot find some portion of the human family ready to denounce as evil: yet were they all ordained in wisdom, and are continued unto us in mercy. The world in which we live has much of evil in it, and, as rational beings, we often have the power of making a choice of evils. Between the evils of slavery, and any of the evil systems of abolition and emancipation which have ever yet been submitted to the American people, we fancy we discover a marked difference--that of slavery being an evil of much less magnitude--attended with fewer unhappy consequences to both races. We would, therefore, act the part of wisdom, and of many evils choose the least--it being the abuse and not the legitimate use of the institutions wisely ordained by God, and sanctioned by human experience, that constitute the evil growing out of them.

Source Citation: Anonymous. "Excerpt from Bible Defense of Slavery: 1." Reproduced in History Resource Center. Farmington Hills, MI: Gale Group.
http://galenet.galegroup.com/servlet/HistRC/
Document Number: CD2152000043

The Rights and the Duties of Masters

SERMON.

COLOSSIANS IV: 1. Masters, give unto your Servants that which is just and equal; knowing that ye also have a master in Heaven.

I REJOICE in the solemnities of this night. I rejoice not merely that a new house has been dedicated to the worship of God and the promulgation of the Gospel: which always affords a just occasion of congratulation and delight, but that a building has been erected--erected in the metropolis of the State, and erected at this particular time, for the special benefit of those who are emphatically the poor of our land. When the scheme was first projected, opposition was very naturally excited to the separation of masters and servants in the solemn offices of religion, which its execution, to some extent, involved. It was felt to be desirable that the different classes of the community should meet together and experience the salutary influence upon their relations to each other, which the contemplation of their common relation to God was suited to exert. These considerations were not destitute of force, and they would have been entitled to prevail, had it not been obvious that the advantages of such promiscuous assemblies were dearly purchased by the exclusion of immense numbers of the coloured population from all adequate opportunities of religious instruction at all. The question was soon found to be partial separation, or a partial diffusion of the gospel among the slaves.

Source Citation: Thornwell, J[ames] H[enley], Rev. The Rights and the Duties of Masters. A Sermon Preached at the Dedication of a Church, Erected in Charleston, S.C., for the Benefit and Instruction of the Coloured Population. Charleston, S.C. Steam Power Press of Walker & James, 1850. Reproduced in History Resource Center. Farmington Hills, MI: Gale Group.
http://galenet.galegroup.com/servlet/HistRC/
Document Number: BT2705230001

Excerpt from *From Darkness Cometh the Light*

Excerpt from *Darkness Cometh the Light, or, Struggles for Freedom*, by Lucy A. Delaney, 1890

... Mrs. Cox was always very severe and exacting with my mother, and one occasion, when something did not suit her, she turned on mother like a fury, and declared, "I am just tired out with the 'white airs' you put on and if you don't behave differently, I will make Mr. Cox sell you down the river at once."

Although mother turned grey with fear, she presented a bold front and retorted that "she didn't care, she was tired of that place, and didn't like to live there, nohow." This so infuriated Mr. Cox that he cried, "How dare a negro say what she liked or what she did not like; and he would show her what he should do."

So, on the day following, he took my mother to an auction-room on Main Street and sold her to the highest bidder, for five hundred and fifty dollars. Oh! God! The pity of it! "In the home of the brave and the land of the free," in the sight of the stars and stripes--that symbol of freedom--sold away from her child, to satisfy the anger of a peevish mistress!

Source Citation: Delaney, Lucy A. "Excerpt of *From Darkness Cometh the Light*." Reproduced in History Resource Center. Farmington Hills, MI: Gale Group.
http://galenet.galegroup.com/servlet/HistRC/
Document Number: CD2161000056

The Annexation of Texas and Its Impact on the United States

Sources from *History Resource Center: U.S.*

Speech of John Quincy Adams

Source Citation: Adams, John Quincy. Speech of John Quincy Adams, of Massachusetts, upon the Right of the People, Men and Women, to Petition: on the Freedom of Speech and of Debate in the House of Representatives of the United States, on the Resolutions of Seven State Legislatures, and the Petitions of More than One Hundred Thousand Petitioners, Relating to the Annexation of Texas to this Union. Delivered in the House of Representatives of the United States, in Fragments of the Morning Hour, from the 16th of June to the 7th of July, 1838, inclusive. Washington: Printed by Gales and Seaton, 1838. Reproduced in History Resource Center. Farmington Hills, MI: Gale Group.
http://galenet.galegroup.com/servlet/HistRC/
Document Number: BT2704900001

This is a speech by John Quincy Adams to the House of Representatives of the United States in 1838. It is an early reference to the question of the annexation of Texas regarding to the divisive issue of slavery.

Annexation, or First Definition of Manifest Destiny

Source Citation: O'Sullivan, John L. "Annexation, or First Definition of Manifest Destiny." Reproduced in History Resource Center. Farmington Hills, MI: Gale Group.
http://galenet.galegroup.com/servlet/HistRC/
Document Number: CD2154000078

In 1845, as war with Mexico loomed over the annexation of Texas, John L. O'Sullivan, editor of *The United States Magazine* and *Democratic Review*, defined this faith in American expansion as the nation's Manifest Destiny.

An Appeal to the People of Massachusetts, on the Texas Question

Source Citation: [Allen, George]. *An Appeal to the People of Massachusetts, on the Texas Question.* Boston: Charles C. Little and James Brown, 1844. Reproduced in History Resource Center. Farmington Hills, MI: Gale Group.
http://galenet.galegroup.com/servlet/HistRC/
Document Number: BT2704320001

This document addresses the question of annexing Texas, which had resurfaced during the presidential election of 1844.

Annexation of Texas

Source Citation: Clay, Henry, et al. Annexation of Texas. *Opinions of Messrs. Clay, Polk, Benton & Van Buren, on the Immediate Annexation of Texas, 1844.* Reproduced in History Resource Center. Farmington Hills, MI: Gale Group.
http://galenet.galegroup.com/servlet/HistRC/
Document Number: BT2700280001

This 1844 letter by Henry Clay, James Polk, Thomas Hart Benton, and Martin Van Buren states opinions on the annexation of Texas.

The Annexation of Texas

Source Citation: *The Annexation of Texas.* Joint Resolution of Congress Annexing Texas to the United States, March 1, 1845. Reproduced in History Resource Center. Farmington Hills, MI: Gale Group. http://galenet.galegroup.com/servlet/HistRC/ Document Number: BT2703810001

This is the official government document declaring the annexation of Texas, *The Joint Resolution of Congress Annexing Texas to the United States, March 1, 1845.*

Editorials Promote War with Mexico and Defy Britain

Source Citation: Whitman, Walt. "Editorials Promote War with Mexico and Defy Britain." Reproduced in History Resource Center. Farmington Hills, MI: Gale Group. http://galenet.galegroup.com/servlet/HistRC/ Document Number: CD2160000195

In 1846-47, poet Walt Whitman edited the Brooklyn *Daily Eagle*, for which he wrote these editorials.

Texas and Oregon. Extract from Polk's Inaugural Address March 4, 1845

Source Citation: Polk, James K. Texas and Oregon. *Extract from Polk's Inaugural Address*, March 4, 1845. Reproduced in History Resource Center. Farmington Hills, MI: Gale Group. http://galenet.galegroup.com/servlet/HistRC/ Document Number: BT2703820001

In 1845, the year James K. Polk assumed the presidency, the doctrine of Manifest Destiny was at its apogee. Polk's inauguration speech displays America's sense of entitlement to and ownership of the West. Enfolding Texas and Oregon into the nation would ensure the spread of peace and democracy—not to mention U.S. territorial hegemony—from coast to coast.

Treaty of Guadalupe Hidalgo

Source Citation: Government, U.S. "Treaty of Guadalupe-Hidalgo." Reproduced in History Resource Center. Farmington Hills, MI: Gale Group. http://galenet.galegroup.com/servlet/HistRC/ Document Number: CD2159000296

This government document, signed in 1848, spelled out the agreement between Mexico and the United States at the end of the Mexican War.

The Great West

Source Citation: Reproduced in History Resource Center. Farmington Hills, MI: Gale Group. http://galenet.galegroup.com/servlet/HistRC/ Document Number: CD2210015148

This picture captures the concept of western expansionism, or Manifest Destiny.

Overview

Texas was part of northern Mexico until 1836. As a result of the Texas Revolution, Texas became an independent republic. As early as 1837, the Republic of Texas sought annexation by the United States, but the United States refused to act.

The two reasons the United States did not annex Texas at that time involved slavery and the possibility of war. Up to that time, western expansion (termed Manifest Destiny in 1845) was extending slavery. Those who disliked slavery considered that the large Texas territory could become several new slave states, with new proslavery senators. There was also a real possibility of war with Mexico if the United States annexed Texas because Mexico still considered Texas as its own territory.

By the presidential election of 1844, the question of annexing Texas loomed large. Henry Clay was nominated by the Whig Party but refused to take a stand on the issue. James K. Polk, nominee of the Democratic Party, was in favor of expanding the territory of the United States and spoke out affirmatively for annexing Texas. Polk won the election. Mexico threatened war, but Congress accepted Texas as a state in 1845 and set the southern boundary at the Rio Grande, 150 miles south of the what most, including Mexico, considered the border. With the border at the Rio Grande, the United States would gain parts of New Mexico and Colorado. Polk offered to buy New Mexico and California from Mexico, but Mexico refused. Polk then led the United States into war with Mexico.

The Mexican War (1846–1848) ended when General Winfield Scott's army occupied Mexico City in September 1847. The Treaty of Guadalupe Hidalgo, effective February 2, 1848, established the Rio Grande as the border between Texas and Mexico. By this treaty, Mexico ceded territory to the United States, which became the states of California, Nevada, Utah, and parts of Colorado, New Mexico, Wyoming, and Arizona. As compensation, the United States paid Mexico $15 million. In addition, the United States paid about $3.25 million for other considerations.

Activities

Focus Activity: Debate

You are one of the four political leaders of the United States presenting your argument on the annexation of Texas to Congress. Prepare a five-minute speech to present on your position.

Use the primary sources that follow to prepare your talk. For additional information, search *History Resource Center: U.S.* using the keywords *annexation of Texas, pro-slavery, anti-slavery,* and *Mexican War*.

Annexation of Texas
The Annexation of Texas

Focus on Writing

Select one of these writing prompts to continue your investigation of the controversy surrounding the annexation of Texas by the United States. Keep in mind the characteristics of the writing mode you choose. Also keep in mind the basic rules of grammar, usage, and mechanics.

Narrative Writing: You are an Anglo living in the Republic of Texas. You left Tennessee and came to Texas seeking a better life for yourself. Write a letter to a friend or family member back in Tennessee giving your views on the possible annexation of Texas by the United States. Include details and facts from the primary sources to make the letter realistic. Include details that tell how you think you will be influenced personally by the decision.

Persuasive Writing: President Polk is said to have provoked war with Mexico in 1846 because of his belief in Manifest Destiny. Write an essay agreeing or disagreeing with the concept of Manifest Destiny. Use information from the primary sources and your background reading to support your position.

Extension

Look through *History Resource Center: U.S.* to locate additional sources that relate to the annexation of Texas. Think about the main topic of this lesson. Think about the sources already listed. This process will help you determine appropriate search words or phrases.

After you have compiled a list of sources, determine the best way to share your findings with your class. The types of sources you find may give you clues about the best method for sharing your findings.

Document-Based Essay Question (DBQ)

The following questions require you to construct a coherent essay that integrates your interpretation of Documents A–I and your knowledge of the period referred to in the questions. Your essay should cite key pieces of evidence from the documents and draw on knowledge of Murrin, Chapter 13, "Manifest Destiny: An Empire for Liberty—or Slavery?"

Analyze the change in position of the United States toward the annexation of Texas between 1837 and 1845 and the results of this change. What played into the U.S. rejection of Texas's early bid for annexation? What changed to allow annexation in 1845? What role did the Mexican War play in these results?

Use the documents and your knowledge of the period 1836–1848 to construct your essay.

Document A

An Appeal to the People of Massachusetts, on the Texas Question

THE course pursued by the Administration in reference to the annexation of Texas renders a crisis inevitable. As the policy is developed,--as its consequences begin to be seriously contemplated,--as the spirit of the movement is clearly manifested,--the people of the Free States will cease to be apathetic, and, under the circumstances which may arise, can hardly fail to become intensely excited. The tone of the Message and of Mr. Calhoun's correspondence has at once deprived the Northern advocates of the measure of the advantage of a prudent and "humbugging" policy. Mr. Calhoun's views have exploded the theory, seized upon with avidity by some who have evidently been desirous of misleading others, that the annexation of Texas might tend to the abolition of slavery. It is now clear that the only design of the measure--the avowed design, too--is, to fortify, extend, and perpetuate the slave-holding power; to insure to the Slave-holding States the control of the General Government for all domestic purposes; and to make the General Government, in their hands, instrumental in effecting a foreign policy which shall place this country in immediate and constant hostility to England upon the great question of universal emancipation, and in reference to all measures and interests connected therewith.

Source Citation: [Allen, George]. *An Appeal to the People of Massachusetts, on the Texas Question.* Boston: Charles C. Little and James Brown, 1844. Reproduced in History Resource Center. Farmington Hills, MI: Gale Group. http://galenet.galegroup.com/servlet/HistRC/
Document Number: BT2704320003

Document B

Speech of John Quincy Adams

TEXAS AND MEXICO.

But the prime cause, and the real object of this war, are not distinctly understood by a large portion of the honest, disinterested, and well-meaning citizens of the United States. Their means of obtaining correct information upon the subject have been necessarily limited; and many of them have been deceived and misled by the misrepresentations of those concerned in it, and especially by hireling writers of the newspaper press. They have been induced to believe that the inhabitants of Texas were engaged in a legitimate contest for the maintenance of the sacred principles of liberty, and the natural, inalienable rights of man:—whereas, the motives of its instigators, and their chief incentives to action, have been, from the commencement, of a directly opposite character and tendency. *It is susceptible of the clearest demonstration, that the immediate cause, and the leading object of this contest, originated in a settled design, among the slaveholders of this country, (with land speculators and slave-traders,) to wrest the large and valuable territory of Texas from the Mexican Republic, in order to re-establish the* SYSTEM OF SLAVERY; *to open a vast and profitable* SLAVE MARKET *therein; and ultimately to annex it to the United States.* And further, it is evident—nay, it is very generally acknowledged— that the insurrectionists are principally citizens of the United States, who have proceeded thither *for the purpose of revolutionizing the* country; and that they are dependant upon this nation, for both the physical and pecuniary means, to carry the design into effect. Whether the national legislature will lend its aid to this most unwarrantable, aggressive attempt, will depend on the VOICE OF THE PEOPLE, expressed in their primary assemblies, *by their petitions* and through the ballot boxes.

The land speculations, aforesaid, have extended to most of the cities and villages of the United States, the British colonies in America, and the settlements of foreigners in all the eastern parts of Mexico. All concerned in them are aware that a change in the government of the country *must* take place, if their claims should ever be legalized.

The advocates of slavery, in our southern states and elsewhere, want more land on this continent suitable for the culture of sugar and cotton: and if Texas, with the adjoining portions of Tamaulipas, Coahuila, Chihuahua, and Santa Fe, east of the Rio Bravo del Norte, can be wrested from the Mexican government, room will be afforded for the redundant slave population in the United States, even to a remote period of time.

Such are the motives for action—such the combination of interests —such the organization, sources of influence, and foundation of authority, upon which the present *Texas Insurrection* rests. The resident colonists compose but a small fraction of the party concerned in it. The standard of revolt was raised as soon as it was clearly ascertained that slavery could not be perpetuated, nor the illegal speculations in land continued, under the *government* of the Mexican Republic. The Mexican authorities were charged with acts of oppression, while the true causes of the revolt—the motives and designs of the insurgents

Source Citation: Adams, John Quincy. Speech of John Quincy Adams, of Massachusetts, upon the Right of the People, Men and Women, to Petition: on the Freedom of Speech and of Debate in the House of Representatives of the United States, on the Resolutions of Seven State Legislatures, and the Petitions of More than One Hundred Thousand Petitioners, Relating to the Annexation of Texas to this Union. Delivered in the House of Representatives of the United States, in Fragments of the Morning Hour, from the 16th of June to the 7th of July, 1838, inclusive. Washington: Printed by Gales and Seaton, 1838. Reproduced in History Resource Center. Farmington Hills, MI: Gale Group.
http://galenet.galegroup.com/serv
Document Number: BT2704900001

Annexation, or First Definition of Manifest Destiny

It is time now for opposition to the Annexation of Texas to cease, all further agitation of the waters of bitterness and strife, at least in connexion with this question,--even though it may perhaps be required of us as a necessary condition of the freedom of our institutions, that we must live on for ever in a state of unpausing struggle and excitement upon some subject of party division or other. But, in regard to Texas, enough has now been given to Party. It is time for the common duty of Patriotism to the Country to succeed;--or if this claim will not be recognized, it is at least time for common sense to acquiesce with decent grace in the inevitable and the irrevocable.

Texas is now ours. Already, before these words are written, her Convention has undoubtedly ratified the acceptance, by her Congress, of our proffered invitation into the Union; and made the requisite changes in her already republican form of constitution to adopt it to its future federal relations. Her star and her stripe may already be said to have taken their place in the glorious blazon of our common nationality; and the sweep of our eagle's wing already includes within its circuit the wide extent of her fair and fertile land.She is no longer to us a mere geographical space--a certain combination of coast, plain, mountain, valley, forest and stream. She is no longer to us a mere country on the map. She comes within the dear and sacred designation of Our Country; no longer a "pays," she is a part of "la patrie;" and that which is at once a sentiment and a virtue, Patriotism, already begins to thrill for her too within the national heart. It is time then that all should cease to treat her as alien, and even adverse--cease to denounce and vilify all and everything connected with her accession--cease to thwart and oppose the remaining steps for its consummation; or where such efforts are felt to be unavailing, at least to embitter the hour of reception by all the most ungracious frowns of aversion and words of unwelcome. There has been enough of all this. It has had its fitting day during the period when, in common with every other possible question of practical policy that can arise, it unfortunately became one of the leading topics of party division, of presidential electioneering. But that period has passed, and with it let its prejudices and its passions, its discords and its denunciations, pass away too. The next session of Congress will see the representatives of the new young State in their places in both our halls of national legislation, side by side with those of the old Thirteen. Let their reception into "the family" be frank, kindly, and cheerful, as befits such an occasion, as comports not less with our own self-respect than patriotic duty towards them. Ill betide those foul birds that delight to 'file their own nest, and disgust the ear with perpetual discord of ill-omened croak.

Source Citation: O'Sullivan, John L. "Annexation, or First Definition of Manifest Destiny." Reproduced in History Resource Center. Farmington Hills, MI: Gale Group.
http://galenet.galegroup.com/servlet/HistRC/
Document Number: CD2154000078

Annexation of Texas

Opinions of Messrs. Clay, Polk, Benton & Van Buren, on the immediate Annexation of Texas.

MR. CLAY'S LETTER.

To the Editors of the National Intelligencer.

RALEIGH, April 17th, 1944.

GENTLEMEN--

Subsequent to my departure from Ashland, in December last, I received various communications from popular assemolages and private individuals, requesting an expression of my opinion upon the question of the annexation of Texas to the United States. I have foreborne to reply to them, because it was not very convenient, during the progress of my journey, to do so, and for other reasons, I did not think it proper unnecessarily to introduce at present a new element among the other exciting subjects which agitate and engross the public mind. The rejection of the overture of Texas, some years ago, to become annexed to the United States, had met with general acquiescence. Nothing has since occurred materially to vary the question. I had seen no evidence of a desire being entertained, on the part of any considerable portion of the American people, that Texas should become an integral part of the United States.

During my sojourn in New-Orleans, I had, indeed, been greatly surprised, by information which I received from Texas, that, in the course of last fall, a voluntary overture had proceeded from the Executive of the United States to the authorities of Texas, to conclude a treaty of annexation; and that, in order to overcome the repugnance felt by any of them to a negotiation upon the subject, strong, and, as I believed, erroneous representations had been made to them, of a state of opinion in the Senate of the United States favourable to the ratification of such a treaty. According to these representations, it had been ascertained that a number of Senators, varying from thirty-five to forty-two, were ready to sanction such a treaty. I was aware, too, that holders of Texas lands and Texas scrip, and speculators in them, were actively engaged in promoting the object of annexation. Still, I did not believe that any Executive of the United States would venture upon so grave and momentous a proceeding, not only without any general manifestation of public opinion in favour of it, but in direct opposition to strong and decided expressions of public disapprobation. But it appears that I was mistaken. To the astonishment of the whole nation, we are now informed that a treaty of annexation has been actually concluded, and is to be submitted to the Senate for its consideration. The motives for my silence, therefore, no longer remain; and I feel it to be my duty to present an exposition of my views and opinions upon the question for what they may be worth, to the public consideration. I adopt this method, as being more convenient than separate replies to the respective communications which I have received.

I regret that I have not the advantage of a view of the treaty itself, so as to enable me to adapt an expression of my opinion to the actual conditions and stipulations which it contains. Not possessing that opportunity, I am constrained to treat the question according to what I presume to be the terms of the treaty. If, without loss of national character, without the hazard of foreign war, with the general concurrence of the nation, without any danger to the integrity of the Union, and without giving an unreasonable price for Texas, the question of annexation were presented, it would appear in quite a different light from that in which, I apprehend, it is now to be regarded.

Document D

The United States acquired a title to Texas, extending as I believe, to the Rio del Norte, by the treaty of Louisiana. They ceded and relinquished that title to Spain by the treaty of 1819, by which the Sabine was substituted for the Rio del Norte as our western boundary. This treaty was negotiated under the administration of Mr. Mouroe, and with the concurrence of his Cabinet, of which Messrs. Crawford, Calhoun and Wirt, being a majority, all southern gentlemen, composed a part. When the treaty was laid before the House of Representatives, being a member of that body, I expressed the opinion which I then entertained, and still hold, that Texas was sacrificed to the acquisition of Florida. We wanted Florida: but I thought it must, from its position, inevitably fall into our possession; that the point of a few years sooner or later was of no sort of consequence, and that in giving five millions of dollars and Texas for it, we gave more than a just equivalent. But if we made a great sacrifice in the surrender of Texas, we ought to take care not to make too great a sacrifice in the attempt to re-acquire it.

My opinions of the inexpediency of the treaty of 1819 did not prevail. The country, and Congress were satisfied with it--appropriations were made to carry it into effect --the line of the Subine was recognised by us as our boundary, in negotiations both with Spain and Mexico, after Mexico became independent, and measures have been in actual progress to mark the line, from the Sabine to the Red River, and thence to the Pacific Ocean. We have thus fairly alienated our title to Texas, by solemn national compacts, to the fulfilment of which we stand bound by good faith and national honour. It is, therefore, perfectly idle and ridiculous, if not dishonourable, to talk of resuming our title to Texas, as if we had never parted with it. We can no more do that than Spain can resume Florida, France Louisiana, or Great Britain the thirteen colonies, now composing a part of the United States.

Source Citation: Clay, Henry, et al. Annexation of Texas. *Opinions of Messrs. Clay, Polk, Benton & Van Buren, on the Immediate Annexation of Texas, 1844*. Reproduced in History Resource Center. Farmington Hills, MI: Gale Group. http://galenet.galegroup.com/servlet/HistRC/
Document Number: BT2700280001
Permission pending

The Great West

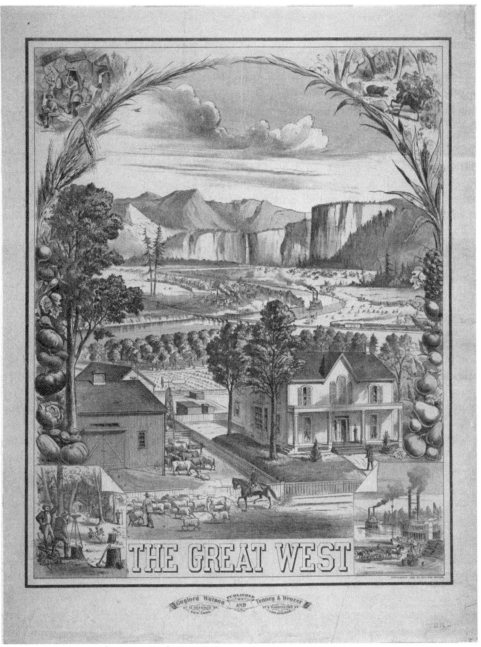

THE GREAT WEST

Courtesy of The Library of Congress, Washington, D.C.

Document F

The Annexation of Texas

Joint Resolution of Congress annexing Texas to the United States

March 1, 1845

(U. S. Statutes at Large, Vol. V, p. 797–8)

Resolved..., That Congress doth consent that the territory properly included within, and rightfully belonging to the Republic of Texas, may be erected into a new State, to be called the State of Texas, with a republican form of government, to be adopted by the people of said republic, by deputies in convention assembled, with the consent of the existing government, in order that the same may be admitted as one of the States of this Union.

2. That the foregoing consent of Congress is given upon the following conditions, and with the following guarantees, to wit: First, Said State to be formed, subject to the adjustment by this government of all questions of boundary that may arise with other governments; and the constitution thereof, with the proper evidence of its adoption by the people of said Republic of Texas, shall be transmitted to the President of the United States, to be laid before Congress for its final action, on or before the first day of January, one thousand eight hundred and forty-six. Second, Said State, when admitted into the Union, after ceding to the United States, all public edifices, fortifications, barracks, ports and harbors, navy and navy-yards, docks, magazines, arms, armaments, and all other property and means pertaining to the public defence belonging to said Republic of Texas, shall retain all the public funds, debts, taxes, and dues of every kind, which may belong to or be due and owing said republic; and shall also retain all the vacant and unappropriated lands lying within its limits, to be applied to the payment of the debts and liabilities of said Republic of Texas, and the residue of said lands, after discharging said debts and liabilities, to be disposed of as said State may direct; but in no event are said debts and liabilities to become a charge upon the Government of the United States. Third. New States, of convenient size, not exceeding four in number, in addition to said State of Texas, and having sufficient population, may hereafter, by the consent of said State, be formed out of the territory thereof, which shall be entitled to admission under the provisions of the federal constitution. And such States as may be formed out of that portion of said territory lying south of thirty-six degrees thirty minutes north latitude, commonly known as the Missouri compromise line, shall be admitted into the Union with or without slavery, as the people of each State asking admission may desire. And in such State or States as shall be formed out of said territory north of said Missouri compromise line, slavery, or involuntary servitude, (except for crime,) shall be prohibited.

3. That if the President of the United States shall in his judgment and discretion deem it most advisable, instead of proceeding to submit the foregoing resolution to the Republic of Texas, as an overture on the part of the United States for admission, to negotiate with that Republic; then,

Be it resolved, That a State, to be formed out of the present Republic of Texas, with suitable extent and boundaries, and with two representatives in Congress, until the next apportionment of representation, shall be admitted into the Union, by virtue of this act, on an equal footing with the existing States, as soon as the terms and conditions of such admission, and the cession of the remaining Texian territory to the United States shall be agreed upon by the Governments of Texas and the United States:

Document F

And that the sum of one hundred thousand dollars be, and the same is hereby, appropriated to defray the expenses of missions and negotiations, to agree upon the terms of said admission and cession, either by treaty to be submitted to the Senate, or by articles to be submitted to the two houses of Congress, as the President may direct.

Source Citation: *The Annexation of Texas*. Joint Resolution of Congress Annexing Texas to the United States, March 1, 1845. Reproduced in History Resource Center. Farmington Hills, MI: Gale Group. http://galenet.galegroup.com/servlet/HistRC/ Document Number: BT2703810001

Document G

Editorials Promote War with Mexico and Defy Britain

May 11, 1846

Yes: Mexico must be thoroughly chastised!--We have reached a point in our intercourse with that country, when prompt and effectual demonstrations of force are enjoined upon us by every dictate of right and policy. The news of yesterday has added the last argument wanted to prove the necessity of an immediate Declaration of War by our government toward its southern neighbor.

We are justified in the face of the world, in having treated Mexico with more forbearance than we have ever yet treated an enemy--for Mexico, though contemptible in many respects, is an enemy deserving a vigorous "lesson." We have coaxed, excused, listened with deaf ears to the insolent gasconnade of her government, submitted thus far to a most offensive rejection of an Ambassador personifying the American nation, and waited for years without payment of the claims of our injured merchants. We have sought peace through every avenue, and shut our eyes to many things, which had they come from England or France, the President would not have dared to pass over without stern and speedy resentment. We have dammed up our memory, of what has passed in the South years ago--of the devilish massacres of some of our bravest and noblest sons, the children not of the South alone, but of the North and West--massacres, not only in defiance of ordinary humanity, but in violation of all the rules of war. Who has read the sickening story of those brutal wholesale murders, so useless for any purpose except gratifying the cowardly appetite of a nation of bravos, willing to shoot down men by the hundred in cold blood--without panting for the day when the prayer of that blood should be listened to--when the vengeance of a retributive God should be meted out to those who so ruthlessly and needlessly slaughtered His image?

Document G

That day has arrived. We think there can be no doubt of the truth of yesterday's news; and we are sure the people here, ten to one, are for prompt and effectual hostilities. Tame newspaper comments, such as appear in the leading Democratic print of today, in New York, and the contemptible anti-patriotic criticisms of its contemporary Whig organ, do not express the sentiments and wishes of the people. Let our arms now be carried with a spirit which shall teach the world that, while we are not forward for a quarrel, America knows how to crush, as well as how to expand!

June 6, 1846

The more we reflect on the matter of annexation as involving a part of Mexico, or even the main bulk of that republic, the more do doubts and obstacles resolve themselves away, and the more plausible appears that, at first blush, most difficult consummation. The scope of our government, (like the most sublime principles of Nature), is such that it can readily fit itself, and extend itself, to almost any extent, and to interests and circumstances the most widely different.

It is affirmed, and with great probability, that in several of the departments of Mexico--the large, fertile and beautiful one of Yucatan, in particular--there is a wide popular disposition to come under the wings of our eagle. The Yucatecos are the best and most industrious citizens in Mexico. They have for years been on bad terms with the central power, and have repeatedly reached open ruptures with the executive and the federal government. The new Congress, which the last accounts mention as having just assembled at Merida, the capital, is acting at the present moment in a manner entirely independent of Mexico--passing tariff laws for itself, and so on. Rumor also states that a mission had been, or is to be, despatched to the United States, with the probable object of treating for annexation or something like it.

Then there is California, in the way to which lovely tract lies Santa Fe; how long a time will elapse before they shine as two new stars in our mighty firmament?

Source Citation: Whitman, Walt. "Editorials Promote War with Mexico and Defy Britain." Reproduced in History Resource Center. Farmington Hills, MI: Gale Group.
http://galenet.galegroup.com/servlet/HistRC/
Document Number: CD2160000195

Texas and Oregon. Extract from Polk's Inaugural Address March 4, 1845

... The Republic of Texas has made known her desire to come into our Union, to form a part of our Confederacy and enjoy with us the blessings of liberty secured and guaranteed by our Constitution. Texas was once a part of our country--was unwisely ceded away to a foreign power--is now independent, and possesses an undoubted right to dispose of a part or the whole of her territory and to merge her sovereignty as a separate and independent state in ours. I congratulate my country that by an act of the late Congress of the United States the assent of this Government has been given to the reunion, and it only remains for the two countries to agree upon the terms to consummate an object so important to both.

I regard the question of annexation as belonging exclusively to the United States and Texas. They are independent powers competent to contract, and foreign nations have no right to interfere with them or to take exceptions to their reunion. Foreign powers do not seem to appreciate the true character of our Government. Our Union is a confederation of independent States, whose policy is peace with each other and all the world. To enlarge its limits is to extend the dominions of peace over additional territories and increasing millions. The world has nothing to fear from military ambition in our Government. While the Chief Magistrate and the popular branch of Congress are elected for short terms by the suffrages of those millions who must in their own persons bear all the burdens and miseries of war, our Government can not be otherwise than pacific. Foreign powers should therefore look on the annexation of Texas to the United States not as the conquest of a nation seeking to extend her dominions by arms and violence, but as the peaceful acquisition of a territory once her own, by adding another member to our confederation, with the consent of that member, thereby diminishing the chances of war and opening to them new and ever-increasing markets for their products.

To Texas the reunion is important, because the strong protecting arm of our Government would be extended over her, and the vast resources of her fertile soil and genial climate would be speedily developed, while the safety of New Orleans and of our whole southwestern frontier against hostile aggression, as well as the interests of the whole Union, would be promoted by it. ...

None can fail to see the danger to our safety and future peace if Texas remains an independent state or becomes an ally or dependency of some foreign nation more powerful than herself. Is there one among our citizens who would not prefer perpetual peace with Texas to occasional wars, which so often occur between bordering independent nations?...

Source Citation: Polk, James K. Texas and Oregon. *Extract from Polk's Inaugural Address*, March 4, 1845. Reproduced in History Resource Center. Farmington Hills, MI: Gale Group.
http://galenet.galegroup.com/servlet/HistRC/
Document Number: BT2703820001
Permission pending

From Treaty of Guadalupe Hidalgo

The United States of America, and the United Mexican States, animated by a sincere desire to put an end to the calamities of the war which unhappily exists between the two Republics, and to establish upon a solid basis relations of peace and friendship, which shall confer reciprocal benefits upon the citizens of both, and assure the concord, harmony and mutual confidence, wherein the two peoples should live, as good neighbours, have for that purpose appointed their respective Plenipotentiaries: that is to say, the President of the United States has appointed Nicholas P. Trist, a citizen of the United States, and the President of the Mexican Republic has appointed Don Luis Gonzaga Cuevas, Don Bernardo Couto, and Don Miguel Atristain, citizens of the said Republic; who, after a reciprocal communication of their respective full powers, have, under the protection of Almighty God, the author of Peace, arranged, agreed upon, and signed the following

Treaty of Peace, Friendship, Limits and Settlement between the United States of America and the Mexican Republic.

Article I.

There shall be firm and universal peace between the United States of America and the Mexican Republic, and between their respective countries, territories, cities, towns and people, without exception of places or persons. ...

Article V.

The Boundary line between the two Republics shall commence in the Gulf of Mexico, three leagues from land, opposite the mouth of the Rio Grande, otherwise called Rio Bravo del Norte, or opposite the mouth of it's deepest branch, if it should have more than one branch emptying directly into the sea; from thence, up the middle of that river, following the deepest channel, where it has more than one, to the point where it strikes the southern boundary of New Mexico; thence, westwardly, along the whole southern boundary of New Mexico (which runs north of the town called Paso) to it's western termination; thence, northward, along the western line of New Mexico, until it intersects the first branch of the river Gila; (or if it should not intersect any branch of that river, then, to the point on the said line interest to such branch, and thence in a direct line to the same;) thence down the middle of the said branch and of the said river, until it empties into the Rio Colorado; thence, across the Rio Colorado, following the division line between Upper and Lower California, to the Pacific Ocean. ...

Article IX.

The Mexicans who, in the territories aforesaid, shall not preserve the character of citizens of the Mexican Republic, conformably with what is stipulated in the preceding article, shall be incorporated into the Union of the United States and be admitted, at the proper time (to be judged of by the Congress of the United States) to the enjoyment of all the rights of citizens of the United States according to the principles of the Constitution; and in the mean time shall be maintained and protected in the free enjoyment of their liberty and property, and secured in the free exercise of their religion without restriction.

Article XII.

In consideration of the extension acquired by the boundaries of the United States, as defined in the fifth Article of the present Treaty, the Government of the United States engages to pay to that of the Mexican Republic the sum of fifteen Millions of Dollars.

Source Citation: Government, U.S. "Treaty of Guadalupe-Hidalgo." Reproduced in History Resource Center. Farmington Hills, MI: Gale Group.
http://galenet.galegroup.com/servlet/HistRC/
Document Number: CD2159000296

Radical Reconstruction and Its Effect on Emancipated Slaves

The First Reconstruction Act, March 2, 1867

Source Citation: *The First Reconstruction Act, March 2, 1867*. Reproduced in History Resource Center. Farmington Hills, MI: Gale Group.
http://galenet.galegroup.com/servlet/HistRC/
Document Number: BT2703920001

This is the legislation for the First Reconstruction Act. President Johnson vetoed this act, but Congress overrode the veto, putting all the states formerly in rebellion under the jurisdiction of five military districts.

Argument for the Impeachment of Andrew Johnson, 1868

Source Citation: "Argument for the Impeachment of Andrew Johnson, 1868." *DISCovering U.S. History*. Gale Research, 1997. Reproduced in History Resource Center. Farmington Hills, MI: Gale Group.
http://galenet.galegroup.com/servlet/HistRC/
Document Number: BT2104210126

This speech called for the impeachment of Andrew Johnson, who came into conflict with members of Congress over the approach to reconstructing the South after the Civil War.

Testimony on Scalawags and Carpetbaggers

Source Citation: Lowe, William M. "Testimony on Scalawags and Carpetbaggers." Reproduced in History Resource Center. Farmington Hills, MI: Gale Group.
http://galenet.galegroup.com/servlet/HistRC/
Document Number: CD2151000035

In this testimony before a Congressional Committee hearing investigating the Ku Klux Klan, a white conservative defines the terms "scalawags" and "carpetbaggers."

Black Code of Mississippi, November, 1865

Source Citation: "Black Code of Mississippi, November, 1865." *DISCovering U.S. History*. Gale Research, 1997. Reproduced in History Resource Center. Farmington Hills, MI: Gale Group.
http://galenet.galegroup.com/servlet/HistRC/
Document Number: BT2104210123

This legislation was passed by the state of Mississippi to limit freedoms of African Americans.

Excerpt from The South: 2

Source Citation: Trowbridge, John. "Excerpt from The South: 2." Reproduced in History Resource Center. Farmington Hills, MI: Gale Group.
http://galenet.galegroup.com/servlet/HistRC/
Document Number: CD2152000515

This is an excerpt from a travel narrative by John Trowbridge, "About Hampton," telling of his visits with freedmen during the summer of 1865.

Civil Rights Act of 1866

Source Citation: "Civil Rights Act of 1866, April 9, 1866." *DISCovering U.S. History*. Gale Research, 1997. Reproduced in History Resource Center. Farmington Hills, MI: Gale Group.
http://galenet.galegroup.com/servlet/HistRC/
Document Number: BT2104210124

This is legislation designed to protect recently freed African Americans from black codes and other repressive state and local legislation.

U.S. Constitution, Fourteenth Amendment

Source Citation: U.S. Congress. "U.S. Constitution, Fourteenth Amendment." Reproduced in History Resource Center. Farmington Hills, MI: Gale Group.
http://galenet.galegroup.com/servlet/HistRC/
Document Number: CD2163000125

This is a copy of the amendment outlining the Congressional plan for postwar reconstruction.

Black Politicians Electioneering in the South

Source Citation: Reproduced in History Resource Center. Farmington Hills, MI: Gale Group.
http://galenet.galegroup.com/servlet/HistRC/
Document Number: CD2210007425

This image shows black politicians electioneering in the South.

Overview

The years following the Civil War were a time of readjustment for the entire nation. The primary focus for the government was on how to incorporate the South back into the Union and transition the slaves to freedom. Unfortunately, much controversy arose over how to proceed with this task.

President Lincoln had anticipated this period of reconstruction, and his plan had been tried in several states in the South before the end of the war. Radicals in Congress, however, were not happy with the plan; they felt Lincoln was not doing enough to change the old order in the South. After Lincoln was assassinated in April 1865, President Johnson took office. Johnson's plan at first pleased the radicals. When Congress reconvened in December 1865, however, it was evident that Johnson's plan was too lenient. Several states even passed laws, known as black codes, that restricted from blacks most of the privileges enjoyed by whites.

Radical members of Congress joined forces with moderate Republicans in 1866 and passed two bills over the veto of Johnson: the Civil Rights Act of 1866 (designed to protect African Americans from the black codes) and the Freedmen's Bureau Bill (extending the life of this federal relief agency). The Reconstruction Act of 1867 divided the South into five military districts to force equality for blacks.

People from the North who went south ("Carpetbaggers") joined with southern white Republicans ("Scalawags") to deal with the problems there. Agents of the Freedmen's Bureau were sent to assist with problems of refugees and the freedmen. This included giving shelter, food, clothing, and medical and legal assistance. The Bureau also doled out abandoned lands and provided schooling. It helped to rebuild roads and restore agricultural production. The Bureau's chief aim was to protect former slaves and give them assistance. Before the war, it was illegal to educate slaves, so the Bureau established schools. They brought teachers, both male and female, in from the North to teach former slaves, both young and old. Many blacks also held political office during this time. Radical Reconstruction was met with great resistance by most southerners.

Reconstruction lasted until about 1877, when the last federal troops were withdrawn from the South. Former slaves were free, but as states reformed their governments, many privileges were lost to the African Americans for another 100 years.

Activities

Focus Activity: Simulation

You are a Radical Republican in Congress. Prepare a five-minute simulation supporting the necessity for taking a strong approach for reconstruction of the South.

Use the primary sources that follow to prepare your simulation. For additional information, search *History Resource Center: U.S.* using the keywords *Radical Republicans, Reconstruction, Andrew Johnson,* and *Civil Rights.*

The First Reconstruction Act, March 2, 1867

Argument for the Impeachment of Andrew Johnson, 1868

Testimony on Scalawags and Carpetbaggers

Black code of Mississippi, November, 1865

Excerpt from the South: 2

Focus on Writing

Select one of these writing prompts to continue your investigation of African Americans during Reconstruction. Keep in mind the characteristics of the writing mode you choose. Also keep in mind the basic rules of grammar, usage, and mechanics.

Narrative Writing: You left your home in the North and came to the Deep South as a teacher in a Freedman's Bureau school (these included white females). Write journal entries for your first few days in your new community. Include details and facts from the primary sources to make the journal realistic. Include details that tell how you feel about the situations you are facing.

Expository Writing: Life for African Americans changed dramatically during Reconstruction. In an essay, compare the lives of African Americans in the South before and after 1865. Use information from the primary sources and your background reading to support your comparison.

Extension

Look through *History Resource Center: U.S.* to locate additional sources that relate to African Americans during Reconstruction. Think about the main topic of this lesson. Think about the sources already listed. This process will help you determine appropriate search words or phrases.

After you have compiled a list of sources, determine the best way to share your findings with your class. The types of sources you find may give you clues about the best method for sharing your findings.

Document-Based Essay Question (DBQ)

The following questions require you to construct a coherent essay that integrates your interpretation of Documents A–H and your knowledge of the period referred to in the questions. Your essay should cite key pieces of evidence from the documents and draw on knowledge of Murrin, Chapter 17, "Reconstruction, 1863–1877."

Analyze Radical Reconstruction as it related to emancipated slaves. Did it accomplish its goals? Were these goals effective?

Use the documents and your knowledge of the period 1863–1877 to construct your essay.

Document A

Black Politicians Electioneering in the South

ELECTIONEERING AT THE SOUTH.—Sketched by W. L. Sheppard.—[See Page 467.]

Courtesy of The Library of Congress, Washington, D.C.

Document B

The First Reconstruction Act, March 2, 1867

WHEREAS no legal State governments or adequate protection for life or property now exists in the rebel States of Virginia, North Carolina, South Carolina, Georgia, Mississippi, Alabama, Louisiana, Florida, Texas, and Arkansas; and whereas it is necessary that peace and good order should be enforced in said States until loyal and republican State governments can be legally established: Therefore,

Be it enacted, That said rebel States shall be divided into military districts and made subject to the military authority of the United States as hereinafter prescribed, and for that purpose Virginia shall constitute the first district; North Carolina and South Carolina the second district; Georgia, Alabama, and Florida the third district; Mississippi and Arkansas the fourth district; and Louisiana and Texas the fifth district.

SEC. 2. That it shall be the duty of the President to assign to the command of each of said districts an officer of the army, not below the rank of brigadier-general, and to detail a sufficient military force to enable such officer to perform his duties and enforce his authority within the district to which he is assigned.

SEC. 3. That it shall be the duty of each officer assigned as aforesaid, to protect all persons in their rights of persons and property, to suppress insurrection, disorder, and violence, and to punish, or cause to be punished, all disturbers of the public peace and criminals; and to this end he may allow local civil tribunals to take jurisdiction of and to try offenders, or, when in his judgment it may be necessary for the trial of offenders, he shall have power to organize military commissions or tribunals for that purpose, and all interference under color of State authority with the exercise of military authority under this act, shall be null and void. ...

Source Citation: The First Reconstruction Act, March 2, 1867. Reproduced in History Resource Center. Farmington Hills, MI: Gale Group.
http://galenet.galegroup.com/servlet/HistRC/
Document Number: BT2703920001
Permission pending

Argument for the Impeachment of Andrew Johnson, 1868

President Andrew Johnson, successor to Lincoln, came into grave conflict with the radical Republicans in Congress over the status of the formerly rebellious states of the South, Johnson being much more willing than Congress to return to those states their antebellum privileges. After Johnson removed Secretary of War Edwin Stanton from office, Congress began impeachment proceedings against him. Johnson was acquitted by one vote.

This is one of the last great battles with slavery. Driven from these legislative chambers, driven from the field of war, this monstrous power has found a refuge in the executive mansion, where, in utter disregard of the Constitution and laws, it seeks to exercise its ancient, far-reaching sway. All this is very plain. Nobody can question it. Andrew Johnson is the impersonation of the tyrannical slave power. In him it lives again. He is the lineal successor of John C. Calhoun and Jefferson Davis; and he gathers about him the same supporters.

Original partisans of slavery, North and South; habitual compromisers of great principles; maligners of the Declaration of Independence; politicians without heart; lawyers for whom a technicality is everything, and a promiscuous company who at every stage of the battle have set their faces against equal rights; these are his allies. It is the old troop of slavery, with a few recruits, ready as of old for violence -- cunning in device and heartless in quibble. With the President at their head, they are now entrenched in the executive mansion. ...

This usurpation, with its brutalities and indecencies, became manifest as long ago as the winter of 1866, when, being President, and bound by his oath of office to preserve, protect, and defend the Constitution, and to take care that the laws are faithfully executed, he took to himself legislative powers in the reconstruction of the Rebel states; and, in carrying forward this usurpation, nullified an act of Congress, intended as the cornerstone of Reconstruction, by virtue of which Rebels are excluded from office under the government of the United States; and, thereafter, in vindication of this misconduct, uttered a scandalous speech in which he openly charged members of Congress with being assassins, and mentioned some by name. Plainly he should have been impeached and expelled at that early day. The case against him was complete. ...

Rebels crawled forth from their retreats. Men who had hardly ventured to expect their lives were now candidates for office, and the rebellion became strong again. The change was felt in all the gradations of government, whether in states, counties, towns, or villages. Rebels found themselves in places of trust, while the truehearted Unionists, who had watched for the coming of our flag and ought to have enjoyed its protecting power, were driven into hiding places. All this was under the auspices of Andrew Johnson. It was he who animated the wicked crew. He was at the head of the work. Loyalty everywhere was persecuted. White and black, whose only offense was that they had been true to their country, were insulted, abused, murdered. There was no safety for the loyal man except within the flash of our bayonets. The story is as authentic as hideous. ...

During these successive assumptions, usurpations, and tyrannies, utterly without precedent in our history, this deeply guilty man ventured upon public speeches, each an offense to good morals, where, lost to all shame, he appealed in coarse words to the coarse passions of the coarsest people, scattering firebrands of sedition, inflaming anew the rebel spirit, insulting good citizens, and, with regard to officeholders, announcing in his own characteristic phrase that he would "kick them out" -- the whole succession of speeches being from their brutalities and indecencies in the nature of a "criminal exposure of his person," indictable at common law, for which no judgment can be too severe. But even this revolting transgression is aggravated when it is considered that through these utterances the cause of justice was imperiled and the accursed demon of civil feud was lashed again into vengeful fury.

All these things from beginning to end are plain facts, already recorded in history and known to all. And it is further recorded in history and known to all, that, through these enormities, any one of which is enough for condemnation, while all together present an aggregation of crime, untold calamities have been brought upon our country; disturbing business and finance; diminishing the national revenues; postponing specie payments; dishonoring the Declaration of Independence in its grandest truths; arresting the restoration of the Rebel states; reviving the dying rebellion, and instead of that peace and reconciliation so much longed for, sowing strife and wrong, whose natural fruit is violence and blood.

For all these, or any one of them, Andrew Johnson should have been impeached and expelled from office. The case required a statement only, not an argument. Unhappily this was not done. As a petty substitute for the judgment which should have been pronounced, and as a bridle on presidential tyranny in "kicking out of office," Congress enacted a law known as the Tenure of Office Act, passed March 2, 1867, over his veto by the vote of two-thirds of both houses. And in order to prepare the way for impeachment, by removing certain scruples of technicality, its violation was expressly declared to be a high misdemeanor. ...

Document D

Testimony on Scalawags and Carpetbaggers, by William M. Lowe, 1872

Question. You have used the epithets "carpet-baggers," and "scalawags," repeatedly, during the course of your testimony. I wish you would give us an accurate definition of what a carpet-bagger is and what a scalawag is.

Answer. Well, sir, the term carpet-bagger is not applied to northern men who come here to settle in the South, but a carpet-bagger is generally understood to be a man who comes here for office sake, of an ignorant or bad character, and who seeks to array the negroes against the whites; who is a kind of political dry-nurse for the negro population, in order to get office through him.

Question. Then it does not necessarily suppose that he should be a northern man?

Answer. Yes, sir; it does suppose that he is to be a northern man, but it does not apply to all northern men that come here.

Question. If he is an intelligent, educated man, and comes here for office, then he is not a carpet-bagger, I understand?

Answer. No, sir; we do not generally call them carpet-baggers. ...

Question. How do you classify Captain Day, who is clerk, I believe, of the district court of the United States, and ex officio commissioner?

Answer. He has never been politically classed. He never took any part in politics at all.

Question. Does he hold office under the Federal Government?

Answer. Yes, sir.

Question. Do you regard him as a carpet-bagger?

Answer. No, sir.

Question. A northern man?

Answer. Yes, sir. ...

Question. What distinguishes him from the genuine carpet-bagger?

Answer. Because he does not associate with the negroes; he does not seek their society, politically or socially; he has nothing to do with them any more than any other white gentleman in the community. ...

Source Citation: Lowe, William M. "Testimony on Scalawags and Carpetbaggers." Reproduced in History Resource Center. Farmington Hills, MI: Gale Group.
http://galenet.galegroup.com/servlet/HistRC/
Document Number: CD2151000035

Black Code of Mississippi, November, 1865

Section 1. All freedmen, free negroes and mulattoes may sue and be sued, implead and be impleaded, in all the courts of law and equity of this State, and may acquire personal property, and choses in action, by descent or purchase, and may dispose of the same in the same manner and to the same extent that white persons may: Provided, That the provisions of this section shall not be so construed as to allow any freedman, free negro or mulatto to rent or lease any lands or tenements except in incorporated cities or towns, in which places the corporate authorities shall control the same.

Section 2. All freedmen, free negroes and mulattoes may intermarry with each other, in the same manner and under the same regulations that are provided by law for white persons: Provided, that the clerk of probate shall keep separate records of the same.

Section 3. All freedmen, free negroes or mullatoes who do now and have herebefore lived and cohabited together as husband and wife shall be taken and held in law as legally married, and the issue shall be taken and held as legitimate for all purposes; and it shall not be lawful for any freedman, free negro or mulatto to intermarry with any white person; nor for any person to intermarry with any freedman, free negro or mulatto; and any person who shall so intermarry shall be deemed guilty of felony, and on conviction thereof shall be confined in the State penitentiary for life; and those shall be deemed freedmen, free negroes and mulattoes who are of pure negro blood, and those descended from a negro to the third generation, inclusive, though one ancestor in each generation may have been a white person.

Section 4. In addition to cases in which freedmen, free negroes and mulattoes are now by law competent witnesses, freedmen, free negroes or mulattoes shall be competent in civil cases, when a party or parties to the suit, either plaintiff or plaintiffs, defendant or defendants; also in cases where freedmen, free negroes and mulattoes is or are either plaintiff or plaintiffs, defendant or defendants. They shall also be competent witnesses in all criminal prosecutions where the crime charged is alleged to have been committed by a white person upon or against the person or property of a freedman, free negro or mulatto: Provided, that in all cases said witnesses shall be examined in open court, on the stand; except, however, they may be examined before the grand jury, and shall in all cases be subject to the rules and tests of the common law as to competency and credibility.

Section 5. Every freedman, free negro and mulatto shall, on the second Monday of January, one thousand eight hundred and sixty-six, and annually thereafter, have a lawful home or employment, and shall have written evidence thereof as follows, to wit: if living in any incorporated city, town, or village, a license from the mayor thereof; and if living outside of an incorporated city, town, or village, from the member of the board of police of his beat, authorizing him or her to do irregular and job work; or a written contract, as provided in Section 6 in this act; which license may be revoked for cause at any time by the authority granting the same.

Section 6. All contracts for labor made with freedmen, free negroes and mulattoes for a longer period than one month shall be in writing, and a duplicate, attested and read to said freedman, free negro or mulatto by a beat, city or county officer, or two disinterested white persons of the county in which the labor is to be performed, of which each party shall have one: and said contracts shall be taken and held as entire contracts, and if the laborer shall quit the service of the employer before the expiration of his term of service, without good cause, he shall forfeit his wages for that year up to the time of quitting.

Document E

Section 7. Every civil officer shall, and every person may, arrest and carry back to his or her legal employer any freedman, free negro, or mulatto who shall have quit the service of his or her employer before the expiration of his or her term of service without good cause; and said officer and person shall be entitled to receive for arresting and carrying back every deserting employee aforesaid the sum of five dollars, and ten cents per mile from the place of arrest to the place of delivery; and the same shall be paid by the employer, and held as a set off for so much against the wages of said deserting employee: Provided, that said arrested party, after being so returned, may appeal to the justice of the peace or member of the board of police of the county, who, on notice to the alleged employer, shall try summarily whether said appellant is legally employed by the alleged employer, and has good cause to quit said employer. Either party shall have the right of appeal to the county court, pending which the alleged deserter shall be remanded to the alleged employer or otherwise disposed of, as shall be right and just; and the decision of the county court shall be final.

Section 8. Upon affidavit made by the employer of any freedman, free negro or mulatto, or other credible person, before any justice of the peace or member of the board of police, that any freedman, free negro or mulatto legally employed by said employer has illegally deserted said employment, such justice of the peace or member of the board of police issue his warrant or warrants, returnable before himself or other such officer, to any sheriff, constable or special deputy, commanding him to arrest said deserter, and return him or her to said employer, and the like proceedings shall be had as provided in the preceding section; and it shall be lawful for any officer to whom such warrant shall be directed to execute said warrant in any county in this State; and that said warrant may be transmitted without endorsement to any like officer of another county, to be executed and returned as aforesaid; and the said employer shall pay the costs of said warrants and arrest and return, which shall be set off for so much against the wages of said deserter.

Section 9. If any person shall persuade or attempt to persuade, entice, or cause any freedman, free negro or mulatto to desert from the legal employment of any person before the expiration of his or her term of service, or shall knowingly employ any such deserting freedman, free negro or mulatto, or shall knowingly give or sell to any such deserting freedman, free negro or mulatto, any food, raiment, or other thing, he or she shall be guilty of a misdemeanor, and, upon conviction, shall be fined not less than twenty-five dollars and not more than two hundred dollars and costs; and if the said fine and costs shall not be immediately paid, the court shall sentence said convict to not exceeding two months imprisonment in the county jail, and he or she shall moreover be liable to the party injured in damages: Provided, if any person shall, or shall attempt to, persuade, entice, or cause any freedman, free negro or mulatto to desert from any legal employment of any person, with the view to employ said freedman, free negro or mullato without the limits of this State, such costs; and if said fine and costs shall not be immediately paid, the court shall sentence said convict to not exceeding six months imprisonment in the county jail.

Section 10. It shall be lawful for any freedman, free negro, or mulatto, to charge any white person, freedman, free negro or mulatto by affidavit, with any criminal offense against his or her person or property, and upon such affidavit the proper process shall be issued and executed as if said affidavit was made by a white person, and it shall be lawful for any freedman, free negro, or mulatto, in any action, suit or controversy pending, or about to be instituted in any court of law equity in this State, to make all needful and lawful affidavits as shall be necessary for the institution, prosecution or defense of such suit or controversy.

Section 11. The penal laws of this state, in all cases not otherwise specially provided for, shall apply and extend to all freedman, free negroes and mulattoes. ...

An Act to Regulate the Relation of Master and Apprentice, as Relates to Freedmen, Free Negroes, and Mulattoes

Section 1. It shall be the duty of all sheriffs, justices of the peace, and other civil officers of the several counties in this State, to report to the probate courts of their respective counties semiannually, at the January and July terms of said courts, all freedmen, free negroes, and mulattoes, under the age of eighteen, in their respective counties, beats, or districts, who are orphans, or whose parent or parents have not the means or who refuse to provide for and support said minors; and thereupon it shall be the duty of said probate court to order the clerk of said court to apprentice said minors to some competent and suitable person on such terms as the court may direct, having a particular care to the interest of said minor: Provided, that the former owner of said minors shall have the preference when, in the opinion of the court, he or she shall be a suitable person for that purpose.

Section 2. The said court shall be fully satisfied that the person or persons to whom said minor shall be apprenticed shall be a suitable person to have the charge and care of said minor, and fully to protect the interest of said minor. The said court shall require the said master or mistress to execute bond and security, payable to the State of Mississippi, conditioned that he or she shall furnish said minor with sufficient food and clothing; to treat said minor humanely; furnish medical attention in case of sickness; teach, or cause to be taught, him or her to read and write, if under fifteen years old, and will conform to any law that may be hereafter passed for the regulation of the duties and relation of master and apprentice: Provided, that said apprentice shall be bound by indenture, in case of males, until they are twenty-one years old, and in case of females until they are eighteen years old.

Section 3. In the management and control of said apprentices, said master or mistress shall have the power to inflict such moderate corporeal chastisement as a father or guardian is allowed to infliction on his or her child or ward at common law: Provided, that in no case shall cruel or inhuman punishment be inflicted.

Section 4. If any apprentice shall leave the employment of his or her master or mistress, without his or her consent, said master or mistress may pursue and recapture said apprentice, and bring him or her before any justice of the peace of the county, whose duty it shall be to remand said apprentice to the service of his or her master or mistress; and in the event of a refusal on the part of said apprentice so to return, then said justice shall commit said apprentice to the jail of said county, on failure to give bond, to the next term of the county court; and it shall be the duty of said court at the first term thereafter to investigate said case, and if the court shall be of opinion that said apprentice left the employment of his or her master or mistress without good cause, to order him or her to be punished, as provided for the punishment of hired freedmen, as may be from time to time provided for by law for desertion, until he or she shall agree to return to the service of his or her master or mistress: Provided, that the court may grant continuances as in other cases: And provided further, that if the court shall believe that said apprentice had good cause to quit his said master or mistress, the court shall discharge said apprentice from said indenture, and also enter a judgment against the master or mistress for not more than one hundred dollars, for the use and benefit of said apprentice, to be collected on execution as in other cases.

Section 5. If any person entice away any apprentice from his or her master or mistress, or shall knowingly employ an apprentice, or furnish him or her food or clothing without the written consent of his or her master or mistress, or shall sell or give said apprentice spirits without such consent, said person so offending shall be guilty of a misdemeanor, and shall, upon conviction there of before the county court, be punished as provided for the punishment of persons enticing from their employer hired freedmen, free negroes or mulattoes.

Section 6. It shall be the duty of all civil officers of their respective counties to report any minors within their respective counties to said probate court who are subject to be apprenticed under the provisions of this act, from time to time as the facts may come to their knowledge, and it shall be the duty of said court from time to time as said minors shall be reported to them, or otherwise come to their knowledge, to apprentice said minors as hereinbefore provided.

Section 9. It shall be lawful for any freedman, free negro, or mulatto, having a minor child or children, to apprentice the said minor child or children, as provided for by this act.

Section 10. In all cases where the age of the freedman, free negro, or mulatto cannot be ascertained by record testimony, the judge of the county court shall fix the age. ...

An Act to Amend the Vagrant Laws of the State

Section 1. All rogues and vagabonds, idle and dissipated persons, beggars, jugglers, or persons practicing unlawful games or plays, runaways, common drunkards, common night-walkers, pilferers, lewd, wanton, or lascivious persons, in speech or behavior, common railers and brawlers, persons who neglect their calling or employment, misspend what they earn, or do not provide for the support of themselves or their families, or dependents, and all other idle and disorderly persons, including all who neglect all lawful business, habitually misspend their time by frequenting houses of ill-fame, gaming-houses, or tippling shops, shall be deemed and considered vagrants, under the provisions of this act, and upon conviction thereof shall be fined not exceeding one hundred dollars, with all accruing costs, and be imprisoned, at the discretion of the court, not exceeding ten days.

Section 2. All freedmen, free negroes and mulattoes in this State, over the age of eighteen years, found on the second Monday in January, 1866, or thereafter, with no lawful employment or business, or found unlawfully assembling themselves together, either in the day or night time, and all white persons assembling themselves with freedmen, free negroes or mulattoes, or usually associating with freedmen, free negroes or mulattoes, on terms of equality, or living in adultery or fornication with a freed woman, freed negro or mulatto, shall be deemed vagrants, and on conviction thereof shall be fined in a sum not exceeding, in the case of a freedman, free negro or mulatto, fifty dollars, and a white man two hundred dollars, and imprisonment at the discretion of the court, the free negro not exceeding ten days, and the white man not exceeding six months. ...

Section 8. Any person feeling himself or herself aggrieved by judgment of any justice of the peace, mayor, or alderman in cases arising under this act, may within five days appeal to the next term of the county court of the proper county, upon giving bond and security in a sum not less than twenty-five dollars nor more than one hundred and fifty dollars, conditioned to appear and prosecute said appeal, and abide by the judgment of the county court; and said appeal shall be tried de novo in the county court, and the decision of the said court shall be final. ...

Civil Rights Act of 1866

Be it enacted …That all persons born in the United States and not subject to any foreign power, excluding Indians not taxed, are hereby declared to be citizens of the United States; and such citizens, of every race and color, without regard to any previous condition of slavery or involuntary servitude, except as a punishment for crime whereof the party shall have been duly convicted, shall have the same right in every State and Territory in the United States, to make and enforce contracts, to sue, be parties, and give evidence, to inherit, purchase, lease, sell, hold, and convey real and personal property, and to full and equal benefit of all laws and proceedings for the security of person and property, as is enjoyed by white citizens, and shall be subject to like punishment, pains, and penalties, and to none other, any law, statute, ordinance, regulation, or custom, to the contrary notwithstanding.

Section 2. And be it further enacted, That any person who, under color or any law, statute, ordinance, regulation, or custom, shall subject, or cause to be subjected, any inhabitant of any State or Territory to the deprivation of any right secured or protected by this act, or to different punishment, pains, or penalties on account of such person having at any time been held in a condition of slavery or involuntary servitude, except as a punishment for crime whereof the party shall have been duly convicted, or by reason of his color or race, than is prescribed for the punishment of white persons, shall be deemed guilty of a misdemeanor, and, on conviction, shall be punished by fine not exceeding one thousand dollars, or imprisonment not exceeding one year, or both, in the discretion of the court. …

Document G

Excerpt from The South: 2

As it was my intention to visit some of the freedmen's settlements in the vicinity, the General kindly placed a horse at my disposal, and I took leave of him. A short gallop brought me to the village of Hampton, distant from the Fortress something over two miles.

"The village of Hampton," says a copy of the "Richmond Examiner" for 1861, "is beautifully situated on an arm of the sea setting in from the adjacent roadstead which bears its name. The late census showed that the aggregate white and black population was nearly two thousand." Some of the residences were of brick, erected at a heavy cost, and having large gardens, out-houses, and other valuable improvements. The oldest building, and the second oldest church in the State, was the Episcopal Church, made of imported brick, and surrounded by a cemetery of ancient graves. "Here repose the remains of many a cavalier and gentlemen, whose names are borne by numerous families all over the Southern States."

The terms which some of these returning Rebels proposed to the freedmen they found in possession of their lands, interested me. One man, whose estate was worth sixteen dollars an acre, offered to rent it to the families living on it for eight dollars an acre, provided that the houses, which they had themselves build, should revert to him at the end of the year. ...

Except on the government farm, where old and infirm persons and orphan children were placed, I did not find anybody who was receiving aid from the government. Said one, "I have a family of seven children. Four are my own, and three are my brother's. I have twenty acres. I get no help from government, and do not want any as long as I can have land." I stopped at another little farm-house, beside which was a large pile of wood, and a still larger heap of unhusked corn, two farm wagons, a market wagon, and a pair of mules. The occupant of this place also had but twenty acres, and he was "getting rich."

Source Citation: Trowbridge, John. "Excerpt from The South: 2." Reproduced in History Resource Center. Farmington Hills, MI: Gale Group.
http://galenet.galegroup.com/servlet/HistRC/
Document Number: CD2152000515

Document H

Civil Rights Act of 1866

Be it enacted …That all persons born in the United States and not subject to any foreign power, excluding Indians not taxed, are hereby declared to be citizens of the United States; and such citizens, of every race and color, without regard to any previous condition of slavery or involuntary servitude, except as a punishment for crime whereof the party shall have been duly convicted, shall have the same right in every State and Territory in the United States, to make and enforce contracts, to sue, be parties, and give evidence, to inherit, purchase, lease, sell, hold, and convey real and personal property, and to full and equal benefit of all laws and proceedings for the security of person and property, as is enjoyed by white citizens, and shall be subject to like punishment, pains, and penalties, and to none other, any law, statute, ordinance, regulation, or custom, to the contrary notwithstanding.

Section 2. And be it further enacted, That any person who, under color or any law, statute, ordinance, regulation, or custom, shall subject, or cause to be subjected, any inhabitant of any State or Territory to the deprivation of any right secured or protected by this act, or to different punishment, pains, or penalties on account of such person having at any time been held in a condition of slavery or involuntary servitude, except as a punishment for crime whereof the party shall have been duly convicted, or by reason of his color or race, than is prescribed for the punishment of white persons, shall be deemed guilty of a misdemeanor, and, on conviction, shall be punished by fine not exceeding one thousand dollars, or imprisonment not exceeding one year, or both, in the discretion of the court. …

Source Citation: "Civil Rights Act of 1866, April 9, 1866." DISCovering U.S. History. Gale Research, 1997. Reproduced in History Resource Center. Farmington Hills, MI: Gale Group.
http://galenet.galegroup.com/servlet/HistRC/
Document Number: BT2104210124

Document I

United States Constitution, Fourteenth Amendment

Passed by Congress June 13, 1866. Ratified July 9, 1868.

Note: Article I, Section 2, of the Constitution was modified by Section 2 of the Fourteenth Amendment.

Section 1. All persons born or naturalized in the United States, and subject to the jurisdiction thereof, are citizens of the United States and of the State wherein they reside. No State shall make or enforce any law which shall abridge the privileges or immunities of citizens of the United States; nor shall any State deprive any person of life, liberty, or property, without due process of law; nor deny to any person within its jurisdiction the equal protection of the laws.

Section 2. Representatives shall be apportioned among the several States according to their respective numbers, counting the whole number of persons in each State, excluding Indians not taxed. But when the right to vote at any election for the choice of electors for President and Vice-President of the United States, Representatives in Congress, the Executive and Judicial officers of a State, or the members of the Legislature thereof, is denied to any of the male inhabitants of such State, being twenty-one years of age and citizens of the United States, or in any way abridged, except for participation in rebellion, or other crime, the basis of representation therein shall be reduced in the proportion which the number of such male citizens shall bear to the whole number of male citizens twenty-one years of age in such State.

Section 3. No person shall be a Senator or Representative in Congress, or elector of President and Vice-President, or hold any office, civil or military, under the United States, or under any State, who, having previously taken an oath, as a member of Congress, or as an officer of the United States, or as a member of any State legislature, or as an executive or judicial officer of any State, to support the Constitution of the United States, shall have engaged in insurrection or rebellion against the same, or given aid or comfort to the enemies thereof. But Congress may by a vote of two-thirds of each House, remove such disability.

Section 4. The validity of the public debt of the United States, authorized by law, including debts incurred for payment of pensions and bounties for services in suppressing insurrection or rebellion, shall not be questioned. But neither the United States nor any State shall assume or pay any debt or obligation incurred in aid of insurrection or rebellion against the United States, or any claim for the loss or emancipation of any slave; but all such debts, obligations and claims shall be held illegal and void.

Section 5. The Congress shall have the power to enforce, by appropriate legislation, the provisions of this article.

Source Citation: U.S. Congress. "U.S. Constitution, Fourteenth Amendment." Reproduced in History Resource Center. Farmington Hills, MI: Gale Group.
http://galenet.galegroup.com/servlet/HistRC/
Document Number: CD2163000125

Manifest Destiny and Native Americans: Conflict on the Great Plains

Sources from *History Resource Center: U.S.*

American Progress

Source Citation: Reproduced in History Resource Center. Farmington Hills, MI: Gale Group.
http://galenet.galegroup.com/servlet/HistRC/
Document Number: CD2210014952

This image depicts the feelings of many Americans during the middle of the nineteenth century.

Across the Continent: Westward the Course of Empire Takes Its Way

Source Citation: Reproduced in History Resource Center. Farmington Hills, MI: Gale Group.
http://galenet.galegroup.com/servlet/HistRC/
Document Number: CD221001514

This image depicts the expansion of white culture across the West during the nineteenth century.

Excerpt from Oration at Plymouth

Source Citation: Adams, John Quincy. "Oration at Plymouth." Reproduced in History Resource Center.
Farmington Hills, MI: Gale Group.
http://galenet.galegroup.com/servlet/HistRC/
Document Number: CD2160000184

This excerpt describes John Quincy Adams's perspective on the relationship between whites and Native Americans.

Excerpt from *A Century of Dishonor*

Source Citation: Jackson, Helen Hunt. "Excerpt from A Century of Dishonor." Reproduced in History
Resource Center. Farmington Hills, MI: Gale Group.
http://galenet.galegroup.com/servlet/HistRC/
Document Number: CD2160000110

This excerpt describes Helen Hunt Jackson's views on the plight of Native Americans in U.S. history.

Curtis Act

Source Citation: Congress, U.S.. "Curtis Act." Reproduced in History Resource Center. Farmington Hills,
MI: Gale Group.
http://galenet.galegroup.com/servlet/HistRC/
Document Number: CD2156000112

This congressional act allows for the protection of Native Americans.

Excerpt from *Black Elk Speaks: Being the Life Story of a Holy Man of the Oglala Sioux*

Source Citation: Black Elk. "Excerpt from Black Elk Speaks." Reproduced in History Resource Center. Farmington Hills, MI: Gale Group.
http://galenet.galegroup.com/servlet/HistRC/
Document Number: CD2164000020

Black Elk gives his views on the relationship between the white soldiers and his people.

Excerpt of The Ghost-Dance Religion and the Sioux Outbreak of 1890

Source Citation: Wovoka. "A Letter from Wovoka." Reproduced in History Resource Center. Farmington Hills, MI: Gale Group.
http://galenet.galegroup.com/servlet/HistRC/
Document Number: CD2164000020

Wovoka describes a Native American ceremony.

Surrender Speech of Chief Joseph

Source Citation: Chief Joseph. "Surrender Speech." Reproduced in History Resource Center. Farmington Hills, MI: Gale Group.
http://galenet.galegroup.com/servlet/HistRC/
Document Number: CD2156000050

Chief Joseph surrenders in this speech.

Testimony Regarding the Effect of Allotment on Indians

Source Citation: Duncan, D.W.C. (Cherokee). "Testimony Regarding the Effect of Allotment on Indians." Reproduced in History Resource Center. Farmington Hills, MI: Gale Group.
http://galenet.galegroup.com/servlet/HistRC/
Document Number: CD2160000067

This testimony describes the effect of a law on the Cherokee Nation.

Overview

Early in our nation's history, the philosophy of expansionism and Native Americans seemed to focus on assimilation through the education of the indigenous peoples to the ways of the Europeans through the mission system and other such activities.

With the rapid growth that came in the early nineteenth century, however, the goal was less the integration of the American Indians and more the extinction.

A series of armed conflicts followed, including the Sand Creek Massacre. In November 1864, Colonel John Chivington led a militia attack on an encampment of Cheyennes and Arapahoes, led by Black Kettle, who had gathered to seek peace. More than 150 men, women, and children were killed.

Native American retaliatory raids followed quickly, as did the signing of more treaties. The U.S. government did not meet the terms of any of these treaties.

On June 25–26, 1876, the Seventh Cavalry, led by Lt. Colonel George Custer, was defeated by a combined force of Cheyenne and Lakota Sioux.

The Dawes Act, passed in 1887, provided for the surveying and dividing of Indian lands into individual allotments, contrary to the native belief in holding land in common. As a result of this law, nearly half of the treaty lands were opened to settlement by non-Indians.

The last major armed battle between the Lakota Sioux and the United States occurred at Wounded Knee on December 29, 1890. A force of 500 members of the Seventh Cavalry surrounded an encampment of Lakota, with orders to escort them to the railroad for removal to Nebraska. Shots were fired, and more than 150 Sioux, many of them women and small children, were killed, along with 25 U.S. soldiers.

Activities

Focus Activity: Congressional Testimony

You are a member of a special commission appointed to determine whether or not the conduct of U.S. military forces has been appropriate in the various conflicts with Native Americans of the Great Plains and the Far West. You will prepare testimony to be presented to Congress with your opinion of the official actions, reasons for that opinion, and your suggestions for future action.

Use the primary sources that follow to prepare your entry. For additional background information, search *History Resource Center: U.S.* using the keywords *Little Bighorn*, *Wounded Knee*, or *Lakota*.

American Progress

Across the Continent: Westward the Course of Empire Takes Its Way

Excerpt from Oration at Plymouth

Excerpt of a Century of Dishonor

Curtis Act, 1898

Excerpt of Black Elk Speaks: Being the Life Story of a Holy Man of the Oglala Sioux

Excerpt of The Ghost-Dance Religion and the Sioux Outbreak of 1890

Chief Joseph's Surrender Speech (1877)

Testimony Regarding the Effect of Allotment on Indians, 1906

Focus on Writing

Select one of the following writing prompts to continue your investigation of the Great Plains Wars. Be sure to follow standard rules of grammar, usage, and mechanics, as well as the characteristics of the writing genre of the assignment.

Narrative Writing: Write a news article that might have been published immediately following one of the following events: Massacre at Sand Creek, Battle of Little Big Horn, or Siege of Wounded Knee. Your article should include all of the "5Ws and 1H" of good journalism: who, what, when, where, why, and how. Include details and events from the primary sources to make the news article realistic.

Persuasive Writing: Native Americans such as Sitting Bull, Chief Joseph, and Geronimo were key leaders during the resistance to white conquest. Imagine that you are one of those leaders, and compose a letter to your people, either to convince them to continue their resistance or to surrender to reservation life. Use information from the primary sources and from your background reading to support your position.

Extension

Look through *History Resource Center: U.S.* to locate additional information about the relations between American Indians and white settlers, as well as the life of the Native Americans after the Plains Wars ended.

After you have completed your research, organize your findings in a creative way in which to share them with your class.

Document-Based Essay Question (DBQ)

The following question requires you to construct a coherent essay that integrates your interpretation of Documents A–G and your knowledge of the period referred to in the question. Your essay should cite key pieces of evidence from the documents and draw on knowledge of Murrin, Chapter 18, "Frontiers of Change, Politics of Stalemate, 1865–1898."

Were the violent conflicts between the American Indians and white settlers in the late nineteenth century the inevitable result of the clash of cultures, or could they have been avoided?

Use the documents and your knowledge of the period 1865–1898 to construct your essay.

Document A

American Progress

Courtesy of The Library of Congress, Washington, D.C.

Source Citation: Reproduced in History Resource Center. Farmington Hills, MI: Gale Group.
http://galenet.galegroup.com/servlet/HistRC/
Document Number: CD2210014952

Across the Continent: Westward the Course of Empire Takes Its Way

Courtesy of The Library of Congress, Washington, D.C.

Excerpt from Oration at Plymouth

No European settlement, ever formed upon this continent, has been more distinguished for undeviating kindness and equity towards the savages. There are, indeed, moralists who have questioned the right of the Europeans to intrude upon the possessions of the aboriginals in any case, and under any limitations whatsoever. But have they maturely considered the whole subject? The Indian right of possession itself stands, with regard to the greatest part of the country, upon a questionable foundation. Their cultivated fields; their constructed habitations; a space of ample sufficiency for their subsistence, and whatever they had annexed to themselves by personal labor, were undoubtedly, by the laws of nature, theirs. But what is the right of a huntsman to the forest of a thousand miles over which he has accidentally ranged in quest of prey? ... Shall the lordly savage not only disdain the virtues and enjoyments of civilization himself, but shall he control the civilization of a world? Shall he forbid the wilderness to blossom like the rose? Shall he forbid the oaks of the forest to fall before the axe of industry, and rise again, transformed into the habitations of ease and elegance? ...No, generous philanthropist! Heaven has not been thus inconsistent in the works of its hands! Heaven has not thus placed at irreconcilable strife, its moral laws with its physical creation! The Pilgrims of Plymouth obtained their right of possession to the territory, on which they settled, by titles as fair and unequivocal as any human property can be held ... The spot on which they fixed had belonged to an Indian tribe, totally extirpated by that devouring pestilence which had swept the country, shortly before their arrival. The territory, thus free from all exclusive possession, they might have taken by the natural right of occupancy. Desirous, however, of giving ample satisfaction to every pretence of prior right, by formal and solemn conventions with the chiefs of the neighboring tribes, they acquired the further security of a purchase. At their hands the children of the desert had no cause of complaint. ...

Source Citation: Adams, John Quincy. "Oration at Plymouth." Reproduced in History Resource Center. Farmington Hills, MI: Gale Group.
http://galenet.galegroup.com/servlet/HistRC/
Document Number: CD2160000184

Document D

Excerpt from *A Century of Dishonor*

... There is not among these three hundred bands of Indians one which has not suffered cruelly at the hands either of the Government or of white settlers. The poorer, the more insignificant, the more helpless the band, the more certain the cruelty and outrage to which they have been subjected. This is especially true of the bands on the Pacific slope. These Indians found themselves of a sudden surrounded by and caught up in the great influx of gold-seeking settlers, as helpless creatures on a shore are caught up in a tidal wave. There was not time for the Government to make treaties; not even time for communities to make laws. The tale of the wrongs, the oppressions, the murders of the Pacific-slope Indians in the last thirty years would be a volume by itself, and is too monstrous to be believed.

It makes little difference, however, where one opens the record of the history of the Indians; every page and every year has its dark stain. The story of one tribe is the story of all, varied only by differences of time and place; but neither time nor place makes any difference in the main facts. Colorado is as greedy and unjust in 1880 as was Georgia in 1830, and Ohio in 1795; and the United States Government breaks promises now as deftly as then, and with an added ingenuity from long practice.

One of its strongest supports in so doing is the wide-spread sentiment among the people of dislike to the Indian, of impatience with his presence as a "barrier to civilization," and distrust of it as a possible danger. The old tales of the frontier life, with its horrors of Indian warfare, have gradually, by two or three generations' telling, produced in the average mind something like an hereditary instinct of unquestioning and unreasoning aversion which it is almost impossible to dislodge or soften. ...

"Why should the Indian be expected to plant corn, fence lands, build houses, or do anything but get food from day to day, when experience has taught him that the product of his labor will be seized by the white man to-morrow? The most industrious white man would become a drone under similar circumstances. Nevertheless, many of the Indians" (the commissioners might more forcibly have said 130,000 of the Indians} "are already at work, and furnish ample refutation of the assertion that 'the Indian will not work.' There is no escape from the inexorable logic of facts. ...

Source Citation: Jackson, Helen Hunt. "Excerpt from A Century of Dishonor." Reproduced in History Resource Center. Farmington Hills, MI: Gale Group.
http://galenet.galegroup.com/servlet/HistRC/
Document Number: CD2160000110

Document E

Curtis Act

An Act for the protection of the people of the Indian Territory, and for other purposes.

... SEC 17. That it shall be unlawful for any citizen of any one of said tribes to inclose or in any manner, by himself or through another, directly or indirectly, to hold possession of any greater amount of lands or other property belonging to any such nation or tribe than that which would be his approximate share of the lands belonging to such nation or tribe and that of his wife and his minor children as per allotment herein provided; and any person found in such possession of lands or other property in excess of his share and that of his family, as aforesaid, or having the same in any manner inclosed, at the expiration of nine months after the passage of this Act, shall be deemed guilty of a misdemeanor ...

Document F

Excerpt from *Black Elk Speaks: Being the Life Story of a Holy Man of the Oglala Sioux*

We wanted a much bigger war-party so that we could meet the soldiers and get revenge. But this was hard, because the people were not all of the same mind, and they were hungry and cold. We had a meeting there, and were all ready to go out with more warriors, when Afraid-of-His-Horses came over from Pine Ridge to make peace with Red Cloud, who was with us there.

Our party wanted to go out and fight anyway, but Red Cloud made a speech to us something like this: "Brothers, this is a very hard winter. The women and children are starving and freezing. If this were summer, I would say to keep on fighting to the end. But we cannot do this. We must think of the women and children and that it is very bad for them. So we must make peace, and I will see that nobody is hurt by the soldiers."

The people agreed to this, for it was true. So we broke camp next day and went down from the O-onagazhee to Pine Ridge, and many, many Lakotas were already there. Also, there were many, many soldiers. They stood in two lines with their guns held in front of them as we went through to where we camped.

And so it was all over.

Document G

Excerpt of The Ghost-Dance Religion and the Sioux Outbreak of 1890

When you get home you must make a dance to continue five days. Dance four successive nights, and the last night keep up the dance until the morning of the fifth day, when all must bathe in the river and then disperse to their homes. You must all do in the same way.

I, Jack Wilson, love you all, and my heart is full of gladness for the gifts you have brought me. When you get home I shall give you a good cloud [rain?] which will make you feel good. I give you a good spirit and give you all good paint. I want you to come again in three months, some from each tribe there [the Indian Territory].

There will be a good deal of snow this year and some rain. In the fall there will be such a rain as I have never given you before.

Grandfather [a universal title of reverence among Indians and here meaning the messiah] says, when your friends die you must not cry. You must not hurt anybody or do harm to anyone. You must not fight. Do right always. It will give you satisfaction in life. This young man has a good father and mother. [Possibly this refers to Casper Edson, the young Arapaho who wrote down this message of Wovoka for the delegation].

I want you to dance every six weeks. Make a feast at the dance and have food that everybody may eat. Then bathe in the water. That is all. You will receive good words again from me some time. Do not tell lies.

Source Citation: Wovoka. "A Letter from Wovoka." Reproduced in History Resource Center. Farmington Hills, MI: Gale Group.
http://galenet.galegroup.com/servlet/HistRC/
Document Number: CD2156000360

Document H

Surrender Speech of Chief Joseph

"I am tired of fighting. Our chiefs are killed. Looking Glass is dead. Toohulhulsote is dead. The old men are all dead. It is the young men who say yes or no. He who led the young men is dead. It is cold and we have no blankets. The little children are freezing to death. My people, some of them, have run away to the hills and have no blankets, no food. No one knows where they are--perhaps freezing to death. I want to have time to look for my children and see how many of them I can find. Maybe I shall find them among the dead. Hear me, my chiefs, I am tired. My heart is sick and sad. From where the sun now stands I will fight no more forever."

Source Citation: Chief Joseph. "Surrender Speech." Reproduced in History Resource Center. Farmington Hills, MI: Gale Group.
http://galenet.galegroup.com/servlet/HistRC/
Document Number: CD2156000050

Document I

Testimony Regarding the Effect of Allotment on Indians

... Before this allotment scheme was put in effect in the Cherokee Nation we were a prosperous people. We had farms. Every Indian in this nation that needed one and felt that he needed one had it. Orchards and gardens--everything that promoted the comforts of private life was ours, even as you--probably not so extensively--so far as we went, even as you in the States. The result has been--which I now want to illustrate, as I set out, by my own personal experience. ...

I am in that fix, Senators; you will not forget now that when I use the word "I" I mean the whole Cherokee people. I am in that fix. What am I to do? I have a piece of property that doesn't support me, and is not worth a cent to me, under the same inexorable, cruel provisions of the Curtis law that swept away our treaties, our system of nationality, our every existence, and wrested out of our possession our vast territory. The same provisions of that Curtis law that ought to have been satisfied with these achievements didn't stop there. The law goes on, and that 60 acres of land, it says, shall not be worth one cent to me; although the Curtis law has given me 60 acres as the only inheritance I have in God's world, even that shall not be worth anything. ...

The Government of the United States knows that these allotments of the Indians are not sufficient. Congress recognizes the fact forcibly, by implication, that these allotments are not sufficient. Why, one American citizen goes out on the western plain in North Dakota to make a home. What is the amount of land allotted to him? Isn't it 160 acres? Why, it is the general consensus all over the country that nothing less would be sufficient to support any family; and there are many years when you think, too, that 160 acres is not sufficient. Since this country has been split up, the Cherokee government abolished, and the allotments attained, immigration has come in from the surrounding States, consisting of persons of different kinds. I have tested them, and know what I am talking about, personally. Persons in pursuit of a sufficient quantity of land upon which to rear their families and take care of themselves. I have interrogated them time and again. I have said to them. "Look here, my friend, where are you going?" "To Indian Territory." "What for?" "To get a piece of land." "Did you have any land in Missouri or Kansas?" "Yes, sir; I had some up there, but it was too small and wasn't sufficient." "How much was it?" "Eighty or one hundred acres," as the case may be; "I have leased out my land up there to parties, and thought I would come down here and get a larger piece of ground." Well, now, that is the state of the case. I think, gentlemen, when you investigate the case fully you will find that these people have been put off with a piece of land that is absolutely inadequate for their needs.

Source Citation: Duncan, D.W.C. (Cherokee). "Testimony Regarding the Effect of Allotment on Indians." Reproduced in History Resource Center. Farmington Hills, MI: Gale Group.
http://galenet.galegroup.com/servlet/HistRC/
Document Number: CD2160000067

Progressivism: Successful Reforms or Middle-Class Delusions?

Sources from *History Resource Center: U.S.*

Sherman Anti-Trust Act Passed, 1890

Source Citation: "*Text of the Sherman Anti-Trust Act*, July 2, 1890." *DISCovering U.S. History*. Gale Research, 1997. Reproduced in History Resource Center. Farmington Hills, MI: Gale Group.
http://galenet.galegroup.com/servlet/HistRC/
Document Number: BT2104241213

This is the text of the Sherman Anti-Trust Act.

I, Candidate for Governor

Source Citation: Sinclair, Upton. "I, Candidate for Governor: 1." Reproduced in History Resource Center. Farmington Hills, MI: Gale Group.
http://galenet.galegroup.com/servlet/HistRC/
Document Number: CD2158000090

This speech gives Upton Sinclair's reasons for running as a candidate for governor of California.

Elizabeth Cady Stanton's Letter to Theodore Roosevelt

Source Citation: Stanton, Elizabeth Cady. "Elizabeth Cady Stanton's Letter to Theodore Roosevelt." Reproduced in History Resource Center. Farmington Hills, MI: Gale Group.
http://galenet.galegroup.com/servlet/HistRC/
Document Number: CD2161000182

Elizabeth Cady Stanton gives an impassioned plea in favor of women's suffrage.

The Seventeenth Amendment

Source Citation: Congress, U.S. "The Seventeenth Amendment." Reproduced in History Resource Center. Farmington Hills, MI: Gale Group.
http://galenet.galegroup.com/servlet/HistRC/
Document Number: CD2155000268

Here is the text of the Seventeenth Amendment, which outlined senate representation in Congress.

The Nineteenth Amendment

Source Citation: Congress, U.S. "The Nineteenth Amendment." Reproduced in History Resource Center. Farmington Hills, MI: Gale Group.
http://galenet.galegroup.com/servlet/HistRC/
Document Number: CD2155000270

Here is the text of the Nineteenth Amendment, which gave women the right to vote.

Keating-Owen Act

Source Citation: "Keating-Owen Act." *American Decades CD-ROM*. Gale Research, 1998. Reproduced in History Resource Center. Farmington Hills, MI: Gale Group.
Document Number: BT2113110145

This act involved important child labor legislation.

Children's Rights Abuses

Source Citation: Reproduced in History Resource Center. Farmington Hills, MI: Gale Group.
http://galenet.galegroup.com/servlet/HistRC/
Document Number: BT2210018752

This poster compares child labor abuses with civil rights abuses committed against African Americans.

Women Learning How to Use a Voting Machine in Chicago

Source Citation: Reproduced in History Resource Center. Farmington Hills, MI: Gale Group.
http://galenet.galegroup.com/servlet/HistRC/
Document Number: CD2210015367

This photograph shows one of the first instances of women voting in the United States.

Overview

At the end of the nineteenth century and the beginning of the twentieth, opportunities for women exploded. Technological advances allowed much more leisure time, while educational opportunities produced a group interested in applying and using the knowledge gained through advanced education.

At the same time, muckrakers and others focused attention on the corruption of machine politics and the social ills plaguing the country, particularly in the rapidly expanding cities. Progressives became concerned with problems of poverty in the tenements, the effects of alcoholism on families, child labor and education, and women's rights, especially the right to vote.

During this time period, monopolies were being attacked through legislation such as the Sherman Anti-Trust Act; regulations were placed on the food, meat, and drug processing/manufacturing industries through the Pure Food and Drug Act and the Meat Inspection Act; and businesses were being discouraged from hiring young children.

Besides these legislative acts, this period saw the ratification of the Seventeenth Amendment, allowing for the direct election of U.S. senators, and the Nineteenth Amendment, extending suffrage to women. The Keating-Owen Act limited child labor, while other legislation policed the behaviors and actions of big business.

Activities

Focus Activity: Hall of Fame Planning Document

Recently, an anonymous philanthropist decided to establish a United States History Hall of Fame to honor those individuals who have made significant contributions to the progress of our nation. You have been hired to be part of a team assigned to develop the wing for the Progressive Movement of the late nineteenth and early twentieth centuries.

As you begin your work, you quickly encounter a problem. There are so many people who were part of the movement, but you have limited space in the museum for your exhibit. Because of this, you will have to limit the number of individuals memorialized.

With your partner, research the individual(s) assigned by your teacher. When you have checked the sources below, write a letter of recommendation for the individual. You will also be "selling" your assigned person to the rest of the team (the class).

Use the primary sources that follow to prepare your Hall of Fame Planning Document. For additional background information, search *History Resource Center: U.S.* using the keywords *progressive* or *Progressive Movement.*

Sherman Antirust Act Passed, 1890

I, Candidate for Governor

Elizabeth Cady Stanton's Letter to Theodore Roosevelt

Keating-Owen Act

Focus on Writing

Select one of the following writing prompts to continue your investigation of the Progressive Era. Be sure to follow standard rules of grammar, usage, and mechanics, as well as the characteristics of the writing genre of the assignment.

Narrative Writing: Upton Sinclair's novel, *The Jungle,* although fiction, played an important role in cleaning up the food and drug industries through the passage of the Pure Food and Drugs Act and the Meat Inspection Act. Choose an issue that was important to the Progressives (or that is important to you) and write a short story, in the style of Sinclair's book, that would focus the attention of readers on the changes needed.

Persuasive Writing: Elizabeth Cady Stanton and Susan B. Anthony, along with many other women, sacrificed a lot to bring the vote to women. However, only about 60 percent of the women eligible to vote did so in the November 2004 elections. Write a speech to convince women that they should participate in the political process by exercising the suffrage won by these progressives.

Extension

During this same time period, many businessmen nicknamed "robber barons" were also involved in philanthropy. Use sources found at *History Resource Center: U.S.* to learn more about these men or about any of the movements from the earlier project.

After you have completed your research, organize your findings in a creative way in which to share them with your class.

Document-Based Essay Question (DBQ)

The following question requires you to construct a coherent essay that integrates your interpretation of Documents A–G and your knowledge of the period referred to in the question. Your essay should cite key pieces of evidence from the documents and draw on knowledge of Murrin, Chapter 20, "An Industrial Society, 1890–1920" and Chapter 21, "Progressivism."

How successful were the Progressives in meeting their goals to remove corruption from government and business?

Use the documents and your knowledge of the period 1890–1920 to construct your essay.

Sherman Anti-Trust Act Passed, 1890

In response to the growth of corporate corruption in the late nineteenth century, the American public demanded greater federal regulation of trusts. The Sherman Anti-Trust Act was passed in an attempt to reduce the unfair practices of big business.

An act to protect trade and commerce against unlawful restraints and monopolies. ...
Be it enacted

SEC. 1. Every contract, combination in the form of trust or otherwise, or conspiracy, in restraint of trade or commerce among the several States, or with foreign nations, is hereby declared to be illegal. Every person who shall make any such contract or engage in any such combination or conspiracy, shall be deemed guilty of a misdemeanor, and, on conviction thereof, shall be punished by fine not exceeding five thousand dollars, or by imprisonment not exceeding one year, or by both said punishments, in the discretion of the court.

SEC. 2. Every person who shall monopolize, or attempt to monopolize, or combine or conspire with any other person or persons, to monopolize any part of the trade or commerce among the several States, or with foreign nations, shall be deemed guilty of a misdemeanor, and, on conviction thereof, shall be punished by fine not exceeding five thousand dollars, or by imprisonment not exceeding one year, or by both said punishments, in the discretion of the court.

SEC. 3. Every contract, combination in form of trust or otherwise, or conspiracy, in restraint of trade or commerce in any Territory of the United States or of the District of Columbia, or in restraint of trade or commerce between any such Territory and another, or between any such Territory or Territories and any State or States or the District of Columbia, or with foreign nations, or between the District of Columbia and any State or States or foreign nations, is hereby declared illegal. Every person who shall make any such contract or engage in any such combination or conspiracy, shall be deemed guilty of a misdemeanor, and, on conviction thereof, shall be punished by fine not exceeding five thousand dollars, or by imprisonment not exceeding one year, or by both said punishments, in the discretion of the court.

SEC. 4. The several circuit courts of the United States are hereby invested with jurisdiction to prevent and restrain violations of this act; and it shall be the duty of the several district attorneys of the United States, in their respective districts, under the direction of the Attorney-General, to institute proceedings in equity to prevent and restrain such violations. Such proceedings may be by way of petition setting forth the case and praying that such violation shall be enjoined or otherwise prohibited. When the parties complained of shall have been duly notified of such petition the courts shall proceed, as soon as may be, to the hearing and determination of the case; and pending such petition and before final decrees, the court may at any time make such temporary restraining order or prohibition as shall be deemed just in the premises.

SEC. 5. Whenever it shall appear to the court before which any proceeding under Section four of this act may be pending, that the ends of justice require that other parties should be brought before the court, the court may cause them to be summoned, whether they reside in the district in which the court is held or not; and subpoenas to that end may be served in any district by the marshal thereof.

SEC. 6. Any property owned under any contract or by any combination, or pursuant to any conspiracy (and being the subject thereof) mentioned in section one of this act, and being in the course of transportation from one State to another, or to a foreign country, shall be

Document A

forfeited to the United States, and may be seized and condemned by like proceedings as those provided by law for the forfeiture, seizure, and condemnation of property imported into the United States contrary to law.

SEC. 7. Any person who shall be injured in his business or property by any other person or corporation by reason of anything forbidden or declared to be unlawful by this act, may sue therefor in any circuit court of the United States in the district in which the defendant resides or is found, without respect to the amount in controversy, and shall recover threefold the damages by him sustained, and the costs of suit, including a reasonable attorney's fee.

SEC. 8. That the word "person," or "persons," wherever used in this act shall be deemed to include corporations and associations existing under or authorized by the laws of either the United States, the laws of any of the Territories, the laws of any State, or the laws of any foreign country.

Source Citation: "*Text of the Sherman Anti-Trust Act*, July 2, 1890." *DISCovering U.S. History*. Gale Research, 1997. Reproduced in History Resource Center. Farmington Hills, MI: Gale Group.
http://galenet.galegroup.com/servlet/HistRC/
Document Number: BT2104241213

Document B

I, **Candidate for Governor**

My Fellow Citizens:

You have seen fit to elect me as your Governor. Under the law approximately sixty days are to elapse before I can take office. In view of the crisis confronting us, it would be a blunder and failure of duty to delay for that long the setting in motion of our declared program.

We have in our State one and a quarter million persons dependent upon public charity. Assuming that each of these persons receives fifty cents per day to live on, our State stands to lose $37,500,000 by sixty days delay in starting the EPIC Plan. We have close to half a million able-bodied workers begging work and unable to find it. Assuming that each of these men by his labor creates four dollars worth of wealth per day, we will lose in that same period the sum of $120,000,000 which might have been created. It ought not to be necessary to present further argument in favor of prompt action.

Source Citation: Sinclair, Upton. "I, Candidate for Governor: 1." Reproduced in History Resource Center. Farmington Hills, MI: Gale Group.
http://galenet.galegroup.com/servlet/HistRC/
Document Number: CD2158000090

Elizabeth Cady Stanton's Letter to Theodore Roosevelt

As you are the first President of the United States who has ever given a public opinion in favor of woman suffrage, and when Governor of New York State, recommended the measure in a message to the Legislature, the members of the different suffrage associations in the United States urge you to advocate in your coming message to Congress, an amendment to the National Constitution for the enfranchisement of American women, now denied their most sacred right as citizens of a Republic.

In the beginning of our nation, the fathers declared that "no just government can be founded without the consent of the governed," and that "taxation without representation is tyranny." Both of these grand declarations are denied in the present position of woman, who constitutes one-half of the people. If "political power inheres in the people"--and women are surely people--then there is a crying need for an amendment to the National Constitution, making these fundamental principles verities.

In a speech made by you at Fitchburg, on Labor Day, you say that you are "in favor of an amendment to the Constitution of the United States, conferring additional power upon the Federal Government to deal with corporations." To control and restrain giant monopolies for the best interests of all the people is of vast import, but of far vaster importance is the establishment and protection of the rights and liberties of one-half the citizens of the United States. Surely there is no greater monopoly than that of all men in denying to all women a voice in the laws they are compelled to obey.

Abraham Lincoln immortalized himself by the emancipation of four million Southern slaves. Speaking for my suffrage coadjutors, we now desire that you, Mr. President, who are already celebrated for so many honorable deeds and worthy utterances, immortalize yourself by bringing about the complete emancipation of thirty-six million women.

With best wishes for your continued honorable career and re-election as President of the United States.

Source Citation: Stanton, Elizabeth Cady. "Elizabeth Cady Stanton's Letter to Theodore Roosevelt." Reproduced in History Resource Center. Farmington Hills, MI: Gale Group.
http://galenet.galegroup.com/servlet/HistRC/
Document Number: CD2161000182

Document D

The Seventeenth Amendment

The Senate of the United States shall be composed of two Senators from each State, elected by the people thereof, for six years; and each Senator shall have one vote. The electors in each State shall have the qualifications requisite for electors of the most numerous branch of the State legislatures.

When vacancies happen in the representation of any State in the Senate, the executive authority of such State shall issue writs of election to fill such vacancies: *Provided*, That the legislature of any State may empower the executive thereof to make temporary appointments until the people fill the vacancies by election as the legislature may direct.

This amendment shall not be so construed as to affect the election or term of any Senator chosen before it becomes valid as part of the Constitution.

Source Citation: Congress, U.S. "The Seventeenth Amendment." Reproduced in History Resource Center. Farmington Hills, MI: Gale Group.
http://galenet.galegroup.com/servlet/HistRC/
Document Number: CD2155000268

Document E

The Nineteenth Amendment

The right of citizens of the United States to vote shall not be denied or abridged by the United States or by any State on account of sex.

Congress shall have power to enforce this article by appropriate legislation.

Source Citation: Congress, U.S. "The Nineteenth Amendment." Reproduced in History Resource Center. Farmington Hills, MI: Gale Group.
http://galenet.galegroup.com/servlet/HistRC/
Document Number: CD2155000270

Document F

Keating-Owen Act

To prevent interstate commerce in the products of child labor, and for other purposes.

Be it enacted by the Senate and House of Representatives of the United States of America in Congress assembled, That no producer, manufacturer, or dealer shall ship or deliver for shipment in interstate or foreign commerce any article or commodity the product of any mine or quarry, situated in the United States, in which within thirty days prior to the time of the removal of such product therefrom children under the age of sixteen years have been employed or permitted to work, or any article or commodity the product of any mill, cannery, workshop, factory, or manufacturing establishment, situated in the United States, in which within thirty days prior to the removal of such product therefrom children under the age of fourteen years have been employed or permitted to work, or children between the ages of fourteen years and sixteen years have been employed or permitted to work more than eight hours in any day, or more than six days in any week, or after the hour of seven o'clock postmeridian, or before the hour of six o'clock antemeridian: *Provided,* That a prosecution and conviction of a defendant for the shipment or delivery for shipment of any article or commodity under the conditions herein prohibited shall be a bar to any further prosecution against the same defendant for shipments or deliveries for shipment of any such article or commodity before the beginning of said prosecution.

Source Citation: "Keating-Owen Act." American Decades CD-ROM. Gale Research, 1998. Reproduced in History Resource Center. Farmington Hills, MI: Gale Group.
Document Number: BT2113110145

Document G

Children's Rights Abuses

This poster parallels children's rights abuses with the civil rights abuses committed against African Americans prior to emancipation.

Document H

Women Learning How to Use a Voting Machine in Chicago

Courtesy of the National Archives

World War I and the Winds of Change
Sources from *History Resource Center: U.S.*

Excerpt from *Women Wanted* (chapter III)

Source Citation: Daggett, Mabel Potter. "Excerpt from *Women Wanted* (chapter III)." Reproduced in History Resource Center. Farmington Hills, MI: Gale Group.
http://galenet.galegroup.com/servlet/HistRC/
Document Number: CD2161000277

This excerpt describes the role played by women during World War I.

The Colored Woman in Industry

Source Citation: Jackson, Mary E. "*The Colored Woman in Industry.*" Reproduced in History Resource Center. Farmington Hills, MI: Gale Group.
http://galenet.galegroup.com/servlet/HistRC/
Document Number: CD2152000161

This source describes the recruitment of black women into industry.

Excerpt from *The War in Its Effect upon Women*

Source Citation: Swanwick, Helena. "Excerpt from The War in Its Effect upon Women." Reproduced in History Resource Center. Farmington Hills, MI: Gale Group.
http://galenet.galegroup.com/servlet/HistRC/
Document Number: CD2164000122

Helen Swanwick shares her views on the effect of war on women.

African-American Girls Laboring in a Brickyard

Source Citation: Reproduced in History Resource Center. Farmington Hills, MI: Gale Group.
http://galenet.galegroup.com/servlet/HistRC/
Document Number: CD2210015313

This photograph depicts a common job held by black girls in the early twentieth century.

Girls Stitching Cloth to Framework of Airplane Wings

Source Citation: Reproduced in History Resource Center. Farmington Hills, MI: Gale Group.
http://galenet.galegroup.com/servlet/HistRC/
Document Number: CD2210015310

This photograph shows how young girls became part of the war effort.

Women Gain the Right to Vote

Source Citation: Reproduced in History Resource Center. Farmington Hills, MI: Gale Group.
http://galenet.galegroup.com/servlet/HistRC/
Document Number: BT2210018692

In 1920, with the ratification of the Nineteenth Amendment to the U.S. Constitution, women gained the right to vote. This photograph depicts its effect on the family.

Marjorie Stinson, World War I Pilot

Source Citation: Reproduced in History Resource Center. Farmington Hills, MI: Gale Group.
http://galenet.galegroup.com/servlet/HistRC/
Document Number: CD2210015407

This picture depicts a female pilot during World War I.

Overview

The period from 1914 through 1920 saw many changes in American society. None of these was more dramatic than that of the role of women.

Women served in the Army and Navy Nursing Corps and answered a call from the U.S. Army Signal Corps for switchboard operators; it was felt that women would be more successful in this role than the men that had earlier held the positions.

On the home front, as nearly five million men enlisted or were drafted into the armed forces, women took up the slack by working in factories and on the farms, doing what had traditionally been considered "man's work." This unprecedented freedom contributed to the women's suffrage movement, which was finally successful in gaining the vote for women with the passage of the Nineteenth Amendment in 1920.

Additionally, women were not willing to return to the kitchen when the soldiers began returning from the war. In fact, the massive number of casualties allowed many women to remain in the workforce. All of this contributed to some major changes in the fabric of American society.

Activities

Focus Activity: War Memorial Design

Washington, D.C., is home to many monuments and memorials to honor individuals and groups who have contributed to our growth and strength as a nation: the World War II memorial, the Iwo Jima memorial, the Vietnam Wall memorial, the Korean War memorial. However, the contributions of women during World War I has been largely forgotten.

You have been commissioned to design a suitable memorial to the women who served with the military as nurses, switchboard operators, and pilots during the Great War. Your design should reflect the facts of their contributions, as well as the impact those contributions had on postwar American society and culture. It may take whatever form you choose but should clearly reflect the information you find during your reading of the resources listed below.

Use the primary sources that follow to prepare your war memorial design. For additional background information, search *History Resource Center: U.S.* using the keywords *Great War* or *World War I*.

Excerpt from *Women Wanted* (chapter III)

The Colored Woman in Industry

Excerpt from *The War in Its Effect upon Women*

African-American Girls Laboring in a Brickyard

Girls Stitching Cloth to Framework of Airplane Wings

Marjorie Stinson, World War I Pilot

Women Gain the Right to Vote

Focus on Writing

Select one of the following writing prompts to continue your investigation of the role of women during World War I. Be sure to follow standard rules of grammar, usage, and mechanics, as well as the characteristics of the writing genre of the assignment.

Expository Writing: As a woman assigned to the Army Nursing Corps or the U.S. Army Signal Corps, write two or three diary entries. Include details and facts from the primary sources to make the diary entries realistic. Remember that diaries are meant to be private, so you can feel free to explore your fears and other feelings about your service, in addition to describing the experience itself.

Persuasive Writing: Using the information you learned from the lesson and what you know about women's contributions on the home front, write a letter to the editor of your local newspaper supporting women's suffrage.

Extension

Locate additional information at *History Resource Center: U.S.* in order to compile a list of women who contributed to the war effort, either overseas or at home, during World War I.

After you have compiled your list of sources and information, organize the results into a meaningful format through which to share your learning with your class.

Document-Based Essay Question (DBQ)

The following question requires you to construct a coherent essay that integrates your interpretation of Documents A–G and your knowledge of the period referred to in the question. Your essay should cite key pieces of evidence from the documents and draw on knowledge of Murrin, Chapter 22, "Becoming a World Power, 1898–1917" and Chapter 23, "War and Society, 1914–1920."

Assess the validity of the following statement: *World War I played a significant role in the changing position of women in American society.*

Use the documents and your knowledge of the period 1898–1920 to construct your essay.

Excerpt from *Women Wanted* (chapter III)

Every man who enlists at that tent near the post office is going to leave a job somewhere whether it's at the factory or the doctor's office or the school teacher's desk, or whether it's your husband. That job will have to be taken by a woman. It's what happened in Europe. It's what now we may see happen here. A great many women will have a wage envelope who never had it before. That may mean affluence to a housefull of daughters. One, two, three, four wages envelopes in a family where father's used to be the only one. You even may have to go out to earn enough to support yourself and the babies. Yes, I know your husband's army pay and the income from investments carefully accumulated through the savings of your married life, will help quite a little. But with the ever rising war cost of living, it may not be enough. It hasn't been for thousands of homes in Europe. And eventually you too may go to work as other women have. It's very strange, is it not, for you of all women who have always believed that women's place was the home. And you may even have been an "anti," a most earnest advocate of an ancient regime against which whole societies and associations of what yesterday were called "advanced" women organised their "suffrage" protests.

To-day no one any longer has to believe what is woman's place. No woman even has anything to say about it. Read everywhere the signs: Women Wanted! Here in New York we are seeing shipload after shipload of men going out to sea in khaki. We don't know how many boat loads like that will go down the bay. But for an army of every million American men in Europe, there must be mobilised another million women to take their places behind the lines here 3,000 miles away from the guns, to carry on the auxiliary operations without which the armies in the field could not exist.

Source Citation: Daggett, Mabel Potter. "Excerpt from *Women Wanted* (chapter III)." Reproduced in History Resource Center. Farmington Hills, MI: Gale Group.
http://galenet.galegroup.com/servlet/HistRC/
Document Number: CD2161000277

The Colored Woman in Industry

Just as colored men are going into the Army, so colored women are being recruited into industry. Thousands and thousands of eager boys have gone to France; we all know about them. Few of us realize that at the same time an army of women is entering mills, factories and all other branches of industry. ..."If you had asked me two years ago about the colored girls as wage earners, in Cleveland, I would have told you that they could be found in housework, as laundresses and cleaning women, as maids, in a few cases in banks and offices, and there were a few employed by a cigar box manufacturing concern.

"Today, however, when I started to list the firms where they were employed, I found that they had entered nearly every field of women's work, and some work where women had not previously been employed. To be sure, at times in small numbers, but they have made an entrance.

"We find them on power sewing machines, making caps, waists, bags and mops; we find them doing pressing and various hand operations in these same shops. They are employed in knitting factories as winders, in a number of laundries on mangles of every type, and in sorting and marking. They are in paper box factories doing both hand and machine work, in button factories on the button machines, in packing houses packing meat, in railroad yards wiping and cleaning engines, and doing sorting in railroad shops. They are found in cigar factories stripping and packing, and in an electrical supply manufacturing plant doing hard work. One of our workers recently found two colored girls on a knotting machine in a bed spring factory, putting the knots in the wire springs."

Source Citation: Jackson, Mary E. "*The Colored Woman in Industry*." Reproduced in History Resource Center. Farmington Hills, MI: Gale Group.
http://galenet.galegroup.com/servlet/HistRC/
Document Number: CD2152000161

Document C

Excerpt from *The War in Its Effect upon Women*

... After the war, men will go on doing what has been regarded as men's work; women, deprived of their own, will also have to do much of what has been regarded as men's work. These things are going to affect women profoundly, and one hopes that the reconstruction of society is going to be met by the whole people -- men and women -- with a sympathetic understanding of each other's circumstances. When what are known as men's questions are discussed, it is generally assumed that the settlement of them depends upon men only; when what are known as women's questions are discussed, there is never any suggestion that they can be settled by women independently of men. Of course they cannot. But, then, neither can "men's questions" be rightly settled so. In fact, life would be far more truly envisaged if we dropped the silly phrases "men's and women's questions"; for, indeed, there are no such matters, and all human questions affect all humanity. ...

Document D

African-American Girls Laboring in a Brickyard

Document E

Girls Stitching Cloth to Framework of Airplane Wings

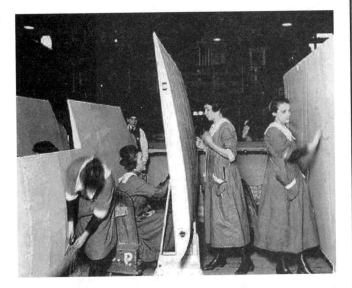

Source Citation: Reproduced in History Resource Center. Farmington Hills, MI: Gale Group. http://galenet.galegroup.com/servlet/HistRC/ Document Number: CD2210015310

Document F

Marjorie Stinson, World War I Pilot

Source Citation: Reproduced in History Resource Center. Farmington Hills, MI: Gale Group. http://galenet.galegroup.com/servlet/HistRC/ Document Number: CD2210015407

Women Gain the Right to Vote

In 1920, with the ratification of the Nineteenth Amendment to the U.S. Constitution, women gained the right to vote.

Courtesy of The Library of Congress, Washington, D.C.

Source Citation: Reproduced in History Resource Center. Farmington Hills, MI: Gale Group.
http://galenet.galegroup.com/servlet/HistRC/
Document Number: BT2210018692

The New Era: Consumer Economy

Sources from *History Resource Center: U.S.*

The New Era Economy

Source Citation: Soule, George. "The New Era Economy." Reproduced in History Resource Center.
Farmington Hills, MI: Gale Group.
http://galenet.galegroup.com/servlet/HistRC/
Document Number: CD2164000198

Economic historian George Soule (1887–1970) summarizes economic developments between 1923 and 1929 in a series of statistical tables.

Labor in the New Era

Source Citation: Goldberg, David J. "Labor in the New Era." Reproduced in History Resource Center.
Farmington Hills, MI: Gale Group.
http://galenet.galegroup.com/servlet/HistRC/
Document Number: CD2164000194

This book examines American industry in the 1920s.

Black Gains in Chicago in the 1920s

Source Citation: Barnett, Claude A. "Black Gains in Chicago in the 1920s." Reproduced in History
Resource Center. Farmington Hills, MI: Gale Group.
http://galenet.galegroup.com/servlet/HistRC/
Document Number: CD2164000182

Chicago, Illinois, is used as a case study on the long-term outcome of the Great Migration in black workers' lives.

Excerpt from *Born in the Country*

Source Citation: Danbom, David B. "Excerpt from *Born in the Country*." Reproduced in History Resource
Center. Farmington Hills, MI: Gale Group.
http://galenet.galegroup.com/servlet/HistRC/
Document Number: CD2164000190

An agricultural historian looks at farmers' problems in the 1920s in a broad historical context.

The Significance of Advertising

Source Citation: Lears, Jackson. "The Significance of Advertising." Reproduced in History Resource
Center. Farmington Hills, MI: Gale Group.
http://galenet.galegroup.com/servlet/HistRC/
Document Number: CD2164000173

Jackson Lears explains the significance of advertising in the 1920s as a delicate balance between a remembered pre-industrial past and the uncertainties of modernity.

Excerpt from *On Being an American*

Source Citation: Mencken, H. L. "Excerpt from On Being an American." Reproduced in History Resource Center. Farmington Hills, MI: Gale Group.
http://galenet.galegroup.com/servlet/HistRC/
Document Number: CD2164000238

H. L. Mencken (1880–1956) writes about the contradictions of progress in the 1920s. He notes the influential role of business, the anti-intellectual tone of the culture, the silliness of some fads, and the ubiquity of materialism.

Excerpt from *Babbitt*

Source Citation: Lewis, Sinclair. "Excerpt from Babbitt." Reproduced in History Resource Center. Farmington Hills, MI: Gale Group.
http://galenet.galegroup.com/servlet/HistRC/
Document Number: CD2164000169

In the novel *Babbitt* (1922), novelist Sinclair Lewis (1885–1951) uses protagonist George F. Babbitt to explore the impact of economic prosperity and mass consumption on middle-class Americans in the 1920s.

A Caricature of 1920s Flapper

Source Citation: Reproduced in History Resource Center. Farmington Hills, MI: Gale Group.
http://galenet.galegroup.com/servlet/HistRC/
Document Number: CD2210015649

This is a caricature showing new personal freedoms and consumer consumption in the 1920s.

Overview

Overall, the 1920s was a decade of dramatic economic growth, and the connection between culture and economy was never more evident. The flapper, a classic symbol of that era, represented not only carefree youth and rebellion but the typical consumer. Several things worked together to create the consumer economy of the 1920s.

Lifestyles changed after World War I. Cities experienced rapid growth, stimulated in part by the Great Migration (African Americans moving to cities from the rural South seeking better incomes and less racism). People no longer made the most of what they consumed or even had social interaction with the people who made those products. Chain stores, such as A&P, brought food and other goods close to the consumer. Assembly-line production allowed for cheaper and more available goods. Incomes, in general, rose, and more people could afford to buy products and housing. The 1920s "flapper" became dependent on an assortment of goods and services, such as cosmetics, tobacco, clothing, and hair salons.

During the 1920s, utility companies brought electric energy into 60 percent of American homes. Having electricity allowed the consumer to use electric appliances, and demand for durable goods such as refrigerators, vacuum cleaners, and radios markedly increased.

One might say that the car led to more changes in the 1920s than anything else. Assembly-line production, introduced by Henry Ford, made cars affordable for the average person. Installment buying came into practice during this time and further increased car sales. Although suburbs were springing up before the 1920s, they grew much faster when people were no longer dependent on trains or trolleys. Cars allowed for personal freedom, and recreational activities, such as traveling or going to the movies, became big businesses. In fact, car sales not only increased significantly between 1916 to 1929, but cars also led to demands for other products, such as glass and rubber. With more cars and trucks in use, the demand rose for all-weather roads. In addition to personal use, auto production created a new way to deliver products to the consumer.

In the vibrant economy of the 1920s, production outpaced demand. The advertising industry grew rapidly by helping to create a desire for these products. Mass produced magazines, such as *Ladies Home Journal* and *Reader's Digest*, contained pages and pages of advertising and were available to rural and urban readers alike.

This decade of prosperity began to collapse in 1929. When the stock market crashed in October 1929, the first stages of the worst depression in U.S. history began.

Activities

Focus Activity: Oral Presentation

You are a present-day historian speaking at a history conference. Prepare a five-minute speech explaining how mass advertising contributed to the development of a consumer-based economy in the 1920s.

Use the primary sources that follow to prepare your talk. For additional information, search **History Resource Center: U.S.** using the keywords *advertising* and *1920s*.

The New Era Economy

Labor in the New Era

The Significance of Advertising

Excerpt from *On Being an American*

Focus on Writing

Select one of these writing prompts to continue your investigation of the consumer economy in the 1920s. Keep in mind the characteristics of the writing mode you choose. Also keep in mind the basic rules of grammar, usage, and mechanics.

Narrative Writing: In *Babbitt*, Sinclair Lewis uses protagonist George F. Babbitt to explore the impact of economic prosperity and mass consumption on middle-class Americans in the 1920s and to give a subtle critique of materialism. Write a short story in which the protagonist helps the reader understand the benefits of the rise of a consumer culture in the 1920s. Use information from the primary sources and from your background reading to make the story realistic.

Expository Writing: The 1920s is considered the "first truly modern decade" and a time of great economic growth. Write an essay that illustrates the effects this had on the consumer. Use information from the primary sources and from your background reading to support your topic.

Extension

Look through **History Resource Center: U.S.** to locate additional sources that relate to the consumer culture of the 1920s. Think about the main topic of this lesson. Think about the sources already listed. This process will help you determine appropriate search words or phrases.

After you have compiled a list of sources, determine the best way to share your findings with your class. The types of sources you find may give you clues about the best method for sharing your findings.

Document-Based Essay Question (DBQ)

The following questions require you to construct a coherent essay that integrates your interpretation of Documents A–I and your knowledge of the period referred to in the questions. Your essay should cite key pieces of evidence from the documents and draw on knowledge of Murrin, Chapter 24, "The 1920s."

Analyze this statement: *The 1920s saw the rise of a consumer-based economy.* What led to this? What were its benefits? Why was it criticized?

Use the documents and your knowledge of the period 1920–1930 to construct your essay.

Document A

The New Era Economy

Economic Developments between 1923 and 1929 are summarized in a series of statistical tables

RECORD OF ECONOMIC CHANGES, UNITED STATES, 1923–1929

POPULATION

Series: Total Unit: Million 1923: 111.91924: 114.11925: 115.81926: 117.41927: 119.01928: 120.51929: 121.8 Percent Change: 9

INCOME OF INDIVIDUALS

INCOME PAYMENTS: Series: Total Unit: Billion $ 1923: 67.91924: 69.1 1925: 72.0 1926: 75.0 1927: 76.1 1928: 77.9 1929: 82.4 Percent Change: 21

RELATIVE SHARE GOING TO HIGHEST:Series: 1 percent of Recipients Unit: Percent 1923: 12.3 1924: 12.9 1925: 13.7 1926: 13.9 1927: 14.4 1928: 14.9 1929: 14.5 Percent Change: 19

NET INCOME AFTER FEDERAL INCOME TAX FOR INCOMES OF: Series: $5,000 Unit: Thousand $ 1923: 4.949 1924: 4.974 1925: 4.992 1926: No Change 1927: No Change 1928: No Change 1929: 4.997 Percent Change: 1

GROSS NATIONAL PRODUCT

TOTAL: Unit: Billion 1929 $ 1923: 78.8 1924: 80.3 1925: 82.9 1926: 88.5 1927: 89.5 1928: 90.6 1929: 97.1 Percent Change: 23

Source Citation: Soule, George. "The New Era Economy." Reproduced in History Resource Center. Farmington Hills, MI: Gale Group.
http://galenet.galegroup.com/servlet/HistRC/
Document Number: CD2164000198

Document B

Labor in the New Era

By 1925, many pundits were proclaiming that the United States had entered a new era of labor-capital peace. They had plenty of evidence to support this belief. Welfare capitalism and other initiatives had apparently made labor content. The industrial surge that began in 1923 provided relatively steady work to factory employees. A low inflation rate erased one of labor's sore points. So few strikes or walkouts occurred that the Department of Labor's Mediation and Conciliation Service (established in 1914 to settle disputes) had little to do.

One of the most remarkable signs of change came in 1923 when the U. S. Steel Corporation voluntarily abandoned the twelve-hour day and adopted three eight-hour shifts. In 1919, Judge Elbert Gary had fought this demand tooth and nail, but by 1923, pressures had mounted on U. S. Steel. Engineers produced studies demonstrating that a shift to the eight-hour day would harm neither productivity nor profits; religious leaders harshly criticized the steel firm's labor policies; Secretary of Commerce Herbert Hoover urged U. S. Steel to abandon this relic of a more ruthless era. Finally Judge Gary acted, and the nation's press hailed this evidence that business had become more responsible and more sensitive to workers' needs.

Giving added substance to the belief that the United States had entered a new era, American industry during the 1920s far outpaced any of its international competitors. Mastering the techniques of mass production, investing heavily in new machinery, and making use of scientific management, American firms achieved astonishing gains in productivity. The greatest growth came in the electrical, rubber, automobile, and machine tool industries, all of which were centered in the Great Lakes region stretching from Buffalo through Cleveland and Detroit to Chicago and Milwaukee. Workers poured into these cities, abandoning farms, small towns, and mining communities. Other parts of the nation appeared stagnant compared to the booming urban Midwest, and the cities' new movie palaces, department stores, skyscrapers, and factories indicated that America had entered a new era--one that many referred to as the Machine Age.

Detroit symbolized both the triumph of the machine and the vibrancy of urban life during the Roaring Twenties. The center of the American automobile industry, its factories attracted whites from Appalachia, African Americans from the Deep South, and immigrants from Mexico. Run at a ruthless pace, its assembly lines burned out many a worker. Its employers, staunch proponents of the open shop, blacklisted any employee suspected of union activity. But workers did not engage in overt protest. If they were dissatisfied, they simply quit and took other jobs. With their earnings they could afford to purchase a Model T, the car that Henry Ford had developed for the masses. Workers with families began to purchase their own homes and, for the first time in their lives, experience the luxury of indoor plumbing. Enjoying the latest dances, dressing in the most up-to-date styles, and purchasing liquor supplied by rumrunners, young workers--known as the "suitcase crowd" because they came and went--gave Detroit a reputation for a lively night life. With money in their pockets, workers flocked to dance halls, ballparks, motion-picture houses, amusement parks, and other places of urban entertainment, and evinced little desire to join labor unions. ...

Source Citation: Goldberg, David J. "*Labor in the New Era.*" Reproduced in History Resource Center. Farmington Hills, MI: Gale Group.
http://galenet.galegroup.com/servlet/HistRC/
Document Number: CD2164000194

Black Gains in Chicago in the 1920s

A decade has passed since the close of the great war, and the general migratory period which brought colored workers north in large numbers to invade fields of labor that were new to them. How nearly the colored laborer is holding his own in the general industrial realm, whether he has made good, whether there is an increasing demand for his labor, the extent to which he has been able to overcome the prejudice which naturally met him from competing whites, how employers regard him, the manner in which unemployment affects him and what the future seems to hold for him are questions which arise as one ponders the record of adventurers.

Chicago, the haven for the largest proportionate share of the influx of southern laborers, offers the most logical proving ground for such a group of inquiries as is contained in the foregoing paragraph.

The Negro population of Chicago was roughly estimated as 45,000 in 1910. It increased 275 per cent in almost direct response to the opportunities which were opened up for work at better wages than those which prevailed on the farms of the South. The pre-war population presented no noteworthy industrial aspects. In fifty years the number of colored citizens had gradually increased without any significant disturbance of their social or economic status.

Before the turn of the century, scions of the eastern line of colored caterers had come to this city and made a place for themselves which lasted for nearly a generation. Sixty per cent of the rest of the inhabitants were confined to jobs of the personal service variety. They were waiters, cooks, maids, porters, janitors. Some of the women were hairdressers and chiropodists, plying their trade among the rich white families.

The number of men and women employed in plants and factories before the war was negligible. The stockyards employed a few colored persons, mixed with Irish and Polish. In factories, however, it was exceptional to see a Negro except as a porter, and that was not the rule. There was a definite spirit of hostility exhibited by the lower class working man, it being unsafe for Negroes to venture alone into their residential districts. This antipathy was almost entirely traceable tot heir desire to keep the Negro from becoming a competitor for the jobs held by white men.

Most of Chicago's new laborers came from Georgia, Mississippi, and Alabama, off the plantations and cotton farms of states that were and are notorious for their small wages, the backwardness of their people, and the vicious character of their laws and treatment of colored people. They were eager to come and the industrialists were eager to get these men and women, but it would have been foolish on the part of any one to have expected these newcomers to fit immediately into the highly-organized and industrialized life of the north. Social problems immediately presented themselves. The turnover of the new Negro labor was high, but, when it was considered that once these farm hands were in northern cities they found greater opportunities for themselves than the labor agents of special interests had held out to them, their desire to get the best possible advantages explains somewhat the waste from turnover for which they were responsible.

Document C

There was an abundance of openings for skilled laborers, but these men and women from the fields were not qualified for the specialized tasks. Most of them were only competent to do the heavy, unskilled work. The industries employing large numbers of Negro workers were: slaughtering, packing of meat, and other food products; iron foundries and iron and steel products; laundries, needle trades; hotels, railroads, Pullman and dining car services, tanneries, taxicab upkeep and repair, and mail order houses. …

Source Citation: Barnett, Claude A. "Black Gains in Chicago in the 1920s." Reproduced in History Resource Center. Farmington Hills, MI: Gale Group.
http://galenet.galegroup.com/servlet/HistRC/
Document Number: CD2164000182

Document D

Excerpt from *Born in the Country*

To the great surprise of many observers, farm prices plunged in the early summer of 1920. Prices stabilized in 1921, then remained relatively flat until after the stock market crash in 1929. When compared with prices during the frothy days of the wartime and postwar eras, prices in the twenties appeared especially low. In 1919, wheat sold for $2.19 per bushel, potatoes went for $2.20 per hundredweight, and cotton fetched $.35 per pound; in 1929 the prices for these products were $1.05, $1.29, and $.17, respectively.

A number of factors contributed to the decline in prices. To a large extent the decline represented a return to a normal supply-and-demand situation following the extraordinary years of the middle and late teens. The artificially high demand on the part of warring and recovering Europeans and Americans had distorted prices. European recovery naturally diminished our exports, but its effects on our international trade were compounded by a major shift in the world financial position of the United States. Before World War I, the United States was a debtor nation. The countries to which it owed money, especially Great Britain, had an incentive to buy American products, because doing so made it possible for the United States to acquire the gold and currency (pounds, in the case of the British) needed to service its debts to them. During the nearly three years of war in which it did not participate, the United States served as supplier and banker to the Allies. In that position, it not only escaped its status as debtor but also became the world's leading creditor. Now the trade shoe was on the other foot. The British needed to sell to the United States to acquire the dollars to service their debts, and they hoped to use as few of those dollars as possible to buy the products the United States had to sell. Consequently, when alternative suppliers were available, the British and others of the United States' debtors preferred to buy from them, and there were alternative suppliers for many agricultural commodities. Europeans began eating more Argentine, Canadian, or Australian wheat, beef, and pork and less of these products from the United States.

Source Citation: Danbom, David B. "Excerpt from *Born in the Country*." Reproduced in History Resource Center. Farmington Hills, MI: Gale Group.
http://galenet.galegroup.com/servlet/HistRC/
Document Number: CD2164000190

The Significance of Advertising

Even at the height of the "prosperity decade," the pilots in the cockpits of modernity were eager to preserve some connection with their imagined preindustrial past. Pseudocolonial artifacts cemented a sense of continuous, coherent group identity.

There was more to this sentiment than yearnings for Anglo-Saxon purity. The most famous folk icons in advertising were black: Rastus, the Cream of Wheat man, and Aunt Jemima. It is easy to dismiss these figures as emblems of white disdain, but their meanings were multivalent. Without question, they epitomized a whole constellation of nurturant values associated with preindustrial household and community life. They provided sustenance; they took care of (white) people. In this they resembled Betty Crocker, the embodiment of old-fashioned neighborliness, created in 1921 by General Mills, or the Mennen Company's Aunt Belle (1920): "Belle is a real person and that is her real name. She really understands babies. She would like to correspond with you about your baby." These figures were created by and for an uprooted suburban bourgeoisie; they may well have helped focus one of the deepest psychic needs of both admakers and their audience: a longing to overcome the sense of separation and loss endemic in a mobile market society, to recreate in fantasy what could not be achieved in everyday life--a renewed connection with the *Gemeinschaftliche* worlds of extended family, local neighborhood, and organic community. The motives of their makers were too numerous to name, but perhaps the basic impulse was an effort to fabricate a stable point of origin for the ever-developing self--though the only materials available might be snippets of memory, half-formed wishes, and cliches from *Life* magazine. As blacks or females (or both), the folk icons fit a familiar role projected for the Other in the white male imagination: like the ideal Victorian woman, they could remain static, sheltering timeless values so that "progressive" men could ignore them in the forward rush to the future. They helped transform certain consumer goods into ballast for the free-floating self.

Still, it would be foolish to treat these motifs as direct expressions of their makers' emotional needs: they were calculated moves in carefully orchestrated campaigns. They were also instances of a rhetorical strategy that has often been employed by American ideologues of progress. No matter how fervently they chanted the gospel of newness, advertisers knew they had to establish some common ground, some sense of old-shoe familiarity between the purchaser and the product. Folk icons served that purpose. They allowed the adepts of progress to have it both ways: to assert that the best of traditional values survived even as modernization whirled ahead at full tilt.

That was the key move in advertising's rhetorical appropriation of the preindustrial past: the innovator presented himself as a traditionalist at heart; the mortal enemy of folklife declared he was its chief defender. This had long been a successful gambit of modernizers, from the federalist orator Tench Coxe to the New South ideologue Henry Grady. But the people who brought this strategy to full fruition were the rhetoricians employed by the modern corporation. In selling home-cooked canned goods, promoting mass-produced craftsmanship, or linking fast-food meals with "family values," twentieth-century advertisers have turned the trick on a scale that Coxe and Grady could hardly have imagined.

By surrounding modern products with a pseudotraditionalist aura, advertisers scrambled past and present, stripped material goods of their actual historical associations, and allowed them to enter a sphere where the object itself was less important than the desires that could be projected onto it. Here as elsewhere, the materialism promoted by advertisers was antimaterial; the success of the corporate economy depended less on the esteem accorded material things than on the constant restimulation of the desire for more of them. The "cult of the transitory," characterized by Henri Lefebvre as "the essence of [capitalist] modernity," promoted a profoundly ambivalent attitude toward material goods: they were something to be longed for, acquired, then superseded and discarded. Planned obsolescence promoted disdain for as well as desire for material goods.

Though the pseudotraditionalist strategy was less direct than the celebration of commodities as status markers for an ever-developing self, the result was the same: goods became floating signifiers, assimilable to the utilitarian purposes of self-salesmanship and the pursuit of success, just as an art that has been reduced to technique becomes assimilable to the needs of advertising. Whether the goods in question signified "old-fashioned convention" or "emancipated modernism," their enlistment in an instrumentalist program transformed a Wildean performance from play to work (or labor, in Hannah Arendt's definition of "making a living").

Yet the appropriation of the past could only succeed as a rhetorical strategy if some traditionalist assumptions (however vague) lingered in the minds of the audience. Something really has been lost in transit to industrial modernity, the ads seem to suggest, some direct, sincere or "folk" quality, and we have miraculously preserved it--authenticity in the midst of artifice, all the charms of yesterday amid the comforts of tomorrow. This effort to supply some psychological ballast for free-floating signifiers suggested that even many advertisers themselves recognized the inadequacy of their progressive program.

Source Citation: Lears, Jackson. "The Significance of Advertising." Reproduced in History Resource Center. Farmington Hills, MI: Gale Group.
http://galenet.galegroup.com/servlet/HistRC/
Document Number: CD2164000173

Document F

Excerpt from *On Being an American*

...So far I go with the fugitive Young Intellectuals—and into the Bad Lands beyond. Such, in brief, are the cardinal articles of my political faith, held passionately since my admission to citizenship and now growing stronger and stronger as I gradually disintegrate into my component carbon, oxygen, hydrogen, phosphorus, calcium, sodium, nitrogen and iron. This is what I believe and preach, *in nomine Domini*, Amen. Yet I remain on the dock, wrapped in the flag, when the Young Intellectuals set sail. Yet here I stand, unshaken and undespairing, a loyal and devoted Americano, even a chauvinist, paying taxes without complaint, obeying all laws that are physiologically obeyable, accepting all the searching duties and responsibilities of citizenship unprotestingly, investing the sparse usufructs of my miserable toil in the obligations of the nation, avoiding all commerce with men sworn to overthrow the government, contributing my mite toward the glory of the national arts and sciences, enriching and embellishing the native language, spurning all lures (and even all invitations) to get out and stay out--here am I, a bachelor of easy means, forty-two years old, unhampered by debts or issue, able to go wherever I please and to stay as long as I please--here am I, contentedly and even smugly basking beneath the Stars and Stripes, a better citizen, I daresay, and certainly a less murmurous and exigent one, than thousands who put the Hon. Warren Gamaliel Harding beside Friedrich Barbarossa and Charlemagne, and hold the Supreme Court to be directly inspired by the Holy Spirit, and belong ardently to every Rotary Club, Ku Klux Klan, and Anti-Saloon League, and choke with emotion when the band plays "The Star-Spangled Banner," and believe with the faith of little children that one of Our Boys, taken at random, could dispose in a fair fight of ten Englishmen, twenty Germans, thirty Frogs, forty Wops, fifty Japs, or a hundred Bolsheviki.

Well, then, why am I still here? Why am I so complacent (perhaps even to the point of offensiveness), so free from bile, so little fretting and indignant, so curiously happy? Why did I answer only with a few academic "Hear, Hears" when Henry James, Ezra Pound, Harold Stearns and the *emigres* of Greenwich Village issued their successive calls to the corn-fed *intelligentsia* to flee the shambles, escape to fairer lands, throw off the curse forever? The answer, of course, is to be sought in the nature of happiness, which tempts to metaphysics. But let me keep upon the ground. To me, at least (and I can only follow my own nose), happiness presents itself in an aspect that is tripartite. To be happy (reducing the thing to its elementals) I must be:

a. Well-fed, unhounded by sordid cares, at ease in Zion.

b. Full of a comfortable feeling of superiority to the masses of my fellow-men.

c. Delicately and unceasingly amused according to my taste

Source Citation: Mencken, H. L. "Excerpt from *On Being an American*." Reproduced in History Resource Center. Farmington Hills, MI: Gale Group.
http://galenet.galegroup.com/servlet/HistRC/
Document Number: CD2164000238

Excerpt from *Babbitt*

There was nothing of the giant in the aspect of the man who was beginning to awaken on the sleeping-porch of a Dutch Colonial house in that residential district of Zenith known as Floral Heights.

His name was George F. Babbitt. He was forty-six years old now, in April, 1920, and he made nothing in particular, neither butter nor shoes nor poetry, but he was nimble in the calling of selling houses for more than people could afford to pay.

His large head was pink, his brown hair thin and dry. His face was babyish in slumber, despite his wrinkles and the red spectacle-dents on the slopes of his nose. He was not fat but he was exceedingly well fed; his cheeks were pads, and the unroughened hand which lay helpless upon the khaki-colored blanket was slightly puffy. He seemed prosperous, extremely married and unromantic; and altogether unromantic appeared this sleeping-porch, which looked on one sizable elm, two respectable grass-plots, a cement driveway, and a corrugated iron garage. Yet Babbitt was again dreaming of the fairy child, a dream more romantic than scarlet pagodas by a silver sea.

For years the fairy child had come to him. Where others saw but Georgie Babbitt, she discerned gallant youth. She waited for him, in the darkness beyond mysterious groves. When at last he could slip away from the crowded house he darted to her. His wife, his clamoring friends, sought to follow, but he escaped, the girl fleet beside him, and they crouched together on a shadowy hillside. She was so slim, so white, so eager! She cried that he was gay and valiant, that she would wait for him, that they would sail--

Rumble and bang of the milk-truck.

Source Citation: Lewis, Sinclair. "Excerpt from *Babbitt*." Reproduced in History Resource Center. Farmington Hills, MI: Gale Group.
http://galenet.galegroup.com/servlet/HistRC/
Document Number: CD2164000169

A Caricature of 1920s Flapper

Source Citation: Reproduced in History Resource Center. Farmington Hills, MI: Gale Group.
http://galenet.galegroup.com/servlet/HistRC/
Document Number: CD2210015649

American Society During the Great Depression

Sources from *History Resource Center: U.S.*

A Hobo Remembers the Great Depression, 1929

Source Citation: "A Hobo Remembers the Great Depression, 1929." *DISCovering U.S. History*. Gale Research, 1997. Reproduced in History Resource Center. Farmington Hills, MI: Gale Group.
http://galenet.galegroup.com/servlet/HistRC/
Document Number: BT2104210026

This is a memoir about life in the Great Depression.

Mr. N.S. to Franklin D. Roosevelt

Source Citation: N.S. (Mr.). "Mr. N.S. to Franklin D. Roosevelt." Reproduced in History Resource Center. Farmington Hills, MI: Gale Group.
http://galenet.galegroup.com/servlet/HistRC/
Document Number: CD2158000163

This letter was sent to FDR during the Great Depression.

Woman's Letter to FDR During the Depression

Source Citation: E.L. (Mrs.). "Woman's Letter to FDR During the Depression." Reproduced in History Resource Center. Farmington Hills, MI: Gale Group.
http://galenet.galegroup.com/servlet/HistRC/
Document Number: CD2161000279

This letter was sent to FDR during the Great Depression.

Mrs. M.H.A. to Eleanor Roosevelt

Source Citation: M.H.A. (Mrs.). "Mrs. M.H.A. to Eleanor Roosevelt." Reproduced in History Resource Center. Farmington Hills, MI: Gale Group.
http://galenet.galegroup.com/servlet/HistRC/
Document Number: CD2158000157

This letter was sent to Eleanor Roosevelt during the Great Depression.

Letter from Impoverished Woman to Eleanor Roosevelt

Source Citation: Unknown. "Letter from Impoverished Woman to Eleanor Roosevelt." Reproduced in History Resource Center. Farmington Hills, MI: Gale Group.
http://galenet.galegroup.com/servlet/HistRC/
Document Number: CD2161000280

This letter was sent to Eleanor Roosevelt during the Great Depression.

Letter to Eleanor Roosevelt Asking for Baby Clothes

Source Citation: H.E.C. (Mrs.). "Letter to Eleanor Roosevelt Asking for Baby Clothes." Reproduced in History Resource Center. Farmington Hills, MI: Gale Group.
http://galenet.galegroup.com/servlet/HistRC/
Document Number: CD2161000281

This letter was sent to Eleanor Roosevelt during the Great Depression.

The Family of an Automobile Worker

Source Citation: Unknown. "The Family of an Automobile Worker." Reproduced in History Resource Center. Farmington Hills, MI: Gale Group.
http://galenet.galegroup.com/servlet/HistRC/
Document Number: CD2158000045

This narrative, written for the Federal Writers' Project of the Works Progress Administration (WPA), relates the experiences of the Whelchel family during the Great Depression.

People Lined Up for Food at a New York City Relief Kitchen

Source Citation: Reproduced in History Resource Center. Farmington Hills, MI: Gale Group.
http://galenet.galegroup.com/servlet/HistRC/
Document Number: CD2210040858

This is a photograph of large numbers of people lined up for food at a New York City relief kitchen during the Depression.

Overview

Most historians consider the Great Depression as lasting from 1929 to about 1939. The 1920s had been an era of overall prosperity. The 1930s, on the other hand, saw the worst economic downturn in United States history. Coupled with the ruinous economic impact of the Great Depression was its equally devastating psychological effect.

During the 1920s, many Americans had come to believe one's success was based on merit. In the beginning years of the Depression, self-blame only added to the problems. In addition, asking for help was extremely humiliating to men who considered themselves to be providers for their families.

The stock market crashed in October 1929. By 1932, nearly one-fourth of Americans were unemployed. Businesses and factories closed their doors, leaving millions out of work. Banks failed, and millions lost their land and life savings. Those who took advantage of the new easy-lending policies of the 1920s could no longer pay for those goods. Farmers had a very difficult time of it. Many had gone into debt to purchase equipment, and a great drought in the early 1930s had turned areas of the country into dust bowls. Farm income dropped 50 percent. Bread lines became a common sight. Poverty was everywhere. Disease brought on by malnutrition flourished. Homelessness was widespread. Many blacks and Native Americans, already living depressed lives, were hit especially hard.

When Franklin D. Roosevelt came into office as president in 1933, he instilled a new optimism in the people by instituting federal relief policies, known as the New Deal. These included the Federal Deposit Insurance Corporation (FDIC), which insured bank deposits, and the Civilian Conservation Corps (CCC), which employed young men 18 to 25 years old to work on various conservation projects. Other programs brought relief to farmers and workers in labor unions. Two projects initiated during the last half of the

1930s (the Second New Deal) were the Works Progress Administration (WPA) and the Social Security Act. The WPA provided people with work, building roads, airports, and schools. Artists worked in separate projects, such as the Federal Writers Project, making records of life during the Depression in words and film. The Social Security Act of 1935 provided insurance for older people.

Even though unemployment still ran about 15 percent in 1939, things began to improve when the United States began expanding its national defense system as World War II broke out in Europe.

Activities

Focus Activity: Interviews

Work in pairs. One of you is a field investigator for the Federal Emergency Relief Administration (FERA). You are interviewing women during the Great Depression to understand what life is like for them, in particular. Prepare a five-minute interview in which the "investigator" will ask questions and the other partner will answer them.

Use the primary sources that follow to prepare your talk. For additional information, search *History Resource Center: U.S.* using the keywords *Great Depression* and *poor women*.

Woman's Letter to FDR During the Depression

Mrs. M.H.A. to Eleanor Roosevelt

Letter from Impoverished Woman to Eleanor Roosevelt

Letter to Eleanor Roosevelt Asking for Baby Clothes

The Family of an Automobile Worker

Focus on Writing

Select one of these writing prompts to continue your investigation of how people managed to survive during the Great Depression. Keep in mind the characteristics of the writing mode you choose. Also keep in mind the basic rules of grammar, usage, and mechanics.

Descriptive Writing: It is the Great Depression, and you have just witnessed your first relief kitchen line. Write an essay about it. Be sure to include both objective and subjective data in your essay. Use information from the primary sources and from your background reading to make the essay realistic.

Expository Writing: Henry Ford's book, *Advice to the Unemployed in the Great Depression,* has just been published. Write a magazine article exploring Ford's suggestions and citing evidence that these suggestions are not always applicable. Use information from the primary sources and from your background reading to support your topic.

Extension

Look through *History Resource Center: U.S.* to locate additional sources that relate to how people survived the hard times of the Great Depression. Think about the main topic of this lesson. Think about the sources already listed. This process will help you determine appropriate search words or phrases.

After you have compiled a list of sources, determine the best way to share your findings with your class. The types of sources you find may give you clues about the best method for sharing your findings.

Document-Based Essay Question (DBQ)

The following questions require you to construct a coherent essay that integrates your interpretation of Documents A–H and your knowledge of the period referred to in the questions. Your essay should cite key pieces of evidence from the documents and draw on knowledge of Murrin, Chapter 24, "The 1920s" and Chapter 25, "The Great Depression and the New Deal, 1929–1939."

Analyze what life was like for many Americans during the Great Depression. What factors contributed to this? To what degree did attitude impact the hardships of daily life?

What measures helped provide relief for these people?

Use the documents and your knowledge of the period 1929–1939 to construct your essay.

Document A

A Hobo Remembers the Great Depression, 1929

The Great Depression was the worst economic crisis in U.S. history. Many, like Louis Banks, were reduced to homelessness.

1929 was pretty hard. I hoboed, I bummed, I begged for a nickel to get somethin' to eat. Go get a job, oh, at the foundry there. They didn't hire me because I didn't belong to the right kind of race. 'Nother time I went into Saginaw, it was two white fellas and myself made three. The fella there hired the two men and didn't hire me. I was back out on the streets. That hurt me pretty bad, the race part.

When I was hoboing, I would lay on the side of the tracks and wait until I could see the train comin'. I would always carry a bottle of water in my pocket and a piece of tape or rag to keep it from bustin' and put a piece of bread in my pocket, so I wouldn't starve on the way. I would ride all day and all night long in the hot sun.

I'd ride atop a boxcar and went to Los Angeles, four days and four nights. The Santa Fe, we'd go all the way with Santa Fe. I was goin' over the hump and I was so hungry and weak 'cause I was goin' into the d.t.'s, and I could see snakes draggin' through the smoke. I was sayin', "Lord, help me, Oh Lord, help me," until a white hobo named Callahan, he was a great big guy, looked like Jack Dempsey, and he got a scissors on me, took his legs and wrapped 'em around me. Otherwise, I was about to fall off the Flyer into a cornfield there. I was sick as a dog until I got into Long Beach, California.

And then I saw a railroad police, a white police. They call him Texas Slim. He shoots you off all trains. We come out of Lima, Ohio ... Lima Slim, he would kill you if he catch you on any train. Sheep train or any kind of merchandise train. He would shoot you off, he wouldn't ask you to get off. ...

Source Citation: "A Hobo Remembers the Great Depression, 1929." *DISCovering U.S. History*. Gale Research, 1997. Reproduced in History Resource Center. Farmington Hills, MI: Gale Group.
http://galenet.galegroup.com/servlet/HistRC/
Document Number: BT2104210026

Document B

Mr. N.S. to Franklin D. Roosevelt

Sulphur Springs, Texas December 11, 1934.

President Roosevelt, Washington, D. C.

Dear President:

I am in debt needing help the worst in the world. I own my own little home and a few live stock. Nine (9) head of red white face cattle and a span of mules. I have them all mortgaged to a man and he is fixing to foreclose me.

I have done all I could to pay the note and have failed on everything I've tried. I fell short on my crop this time and he didn't allow me even one nickle out of it to feed myself while I was gathering it and now winter is here and I have a wife and three (3) little children, haven't got clothes enough to hardly keep them from freezing. My house got burned up three years ago and I'm living in just a hole of a house and we are in a suffering condition. My little children talking about Santa Claus and I hate to see Xmas come this time because I know it will be one of the dullest Xmas they ever witnessed.

I have tried to compromise with the man that I am in debt to and he wont except nothing but the money or my stock and I can't borrow the money and I need my stock so I am asking you for help of some kind please.

So I remain,

Your humble servant, N.S. Sulphur Springs, Texas.

P.S. That man won't even agree for me to have my stock fed.

Source Citation: N.S. (Mr.). "Mr. N.S. to Franklin D. Roosevelt." Reproduced in History Resource Center. Farmington Hills, MI: Gale Group.
http://galenet.galegroup.com/servlet/HistRC/
Document Number: CD2158000163

Document C

Woman's Letter to FDR During the Depression

Letter to Franklin D. Roosevelt Phila., Pa. November 26, 1934

Dear Mr. President:

I am forced to write to you because we find ourselves in a very serious condition. For the last three or four years we have had depression and suffered with my family and little children severely. Now Since the Home Owners Loan Corporation opened up, I have been going there in order to save my home, because there has been unemployment in my home more than three years. You can imagine that I and my family have suffered from lack of water supply in my house for more than two years. Last winter I did not have coal and the pipes burst in my house and therefore could not make heat in the house. Now winter is here again and we are suffering of cold, no water in the house, and we are facing to be forced out of the house, because I have no money to move or pay so much money as they want when after making settlement I am mother of little children, am sick and losing my health, and we are eight people in the family, and where can I go when I don't have money because no one is working in my house. The Home Loan Corporation wants $42, a month rent or else we will have to be on the street. I am living in this house for about ten years and when times were good we would put our last cent in the house and now I have no money, no home and nowheres to go. I beg of you to please help me and my family and little children for the sake of a sick mother and suffering family to give this your immediate attention so we will not be forced to move or put out in the street.

Waiting and Hoping that you will act quickly.

Thanking you very much I remain

Mrs. E. L.

Source Citation: E.L. (Mrs.). "Woman's Letter to FDR During the Depression." Reproduced in History Resource Center. Farmington Hills, MI: Gale Group.
http://galenet.galegroup.com/servlet/HistRC/
Document Number: CD2161000279

Mrs. M.H.A. to Eleanor Roosevelt

Eureka, Calif. June 14, 1934

Mrs. F. D. RooseveltWashington, D. C.

Dear Mrs. Roosevelt:

I know you are overburdened with requests for help and if my plea cannot be recognized, I'll understand it is because you have so many others, all of them worthy.

But I am not asking for myself alone. It is as a potential mother and as one woman to another.

My husband and I are a young couple of very simple, almost poor families. We married eight years ago on the proverbial shoe-string but with a wealth of love. We both wanted more than anything else to establish a home and maintain that home in a charming, quiet manner. I had a job in the County Court House before I married and my husband was, and is, a surveyor. I kept my job as it seemed the best and only way for us to pay for a home as quickly as we could. His work was not always permanent, as surveyors jobs seldom are, but we managed to build our home and furnish it comfortably. Perhaps we were foolish to put all our money into it but we felt it was not only a pleasure but a saving for the future.

Then came the depression. My work has continued and my salary alone has just been sufficient to make our monthly payments on the house and keep our bills paid. But with the exception of two and one-half months work with the U.S. Coast and Geodetic Survey under the C.W.A, my husband has not had work since August, 1932.

My salary could continue to keep us going, but--I am to have a baby. We wanted one before but felt we should have more assurance for the future before we deliberately took such a responsibility. But now that it has happened, I won't give it up! I'm willing to undergo any hardship for myself and I can get a leave of absence from my job for a year. But can't you, won't you do something so my husband can have a job, at least during that year? I realize there is going to be a lot of expense and we have absolutely nothing but our home which still carries a mortgage of $2000. We can't lose that because our baby will need it. And I can't wait until the depression is over to have a baby. I will be 31 in October and I'll soon be too old.

We had such high hopes in the early spring that the Coast and Geodetic work would continue. Tommy, my husband, had a good position there, and we were so happy. We thought surely our dreams of a family could come true. Then the work ended and like "The best laid plans of mice and men" our hopes were crushed again. But now Fate has taken it into her own hands and left us to work it out somehow. I'm happy, of course, but Tommy is nearly out of his head. He has tried every conceivable prospect but you must know how even pick and shovel jobs do not exist.

If the Coast and Geodetic work could continue or if he could get a job with the Bureau of Public Roads, - anything in the surveying line. A year is all I ask and after that I can go back to work and we can work out our own salvation. But to have this baby come to a home full of worry and despair, with no money for things it needs, is not fair. It needs and deserves a happy start in life.

As I said before, if it were only ourselves, or if there were something we could do about it, we would never ask for help. We have always stood on our own feet and been proud and happy. But you are a mother and you'll understand this crisis.

Document D

Tommy is competent and dependable. He has a surveyor's license and was level man for the U.S. Coast and Geodetic work in this (Humboldt) county. He will go away from home for work. if necessary, but, dear Mrs. Roosevelt, will you see if you can arrange for a job for him? It sounds impossible, I know, but I am at a point where I *ask* the impossible. I have to be selfish now.

I shall hope and pray for a reply and tell myself that you are the busiest woman in America, if I don't receive it. I am going to continue to work as long as I can and then- an interval of waiting. God grant it will be serene and untroubled for my baby's sake.

Very sincerely yours,

Mrs. M. H. A. Eureka, Humboldt County, California

Source Citation: M.H.A. (Mrs.). "Mrs. M.H.A. to Eleanor Roosevelt." Reproduced in History Resource Center. Farmington Hills, MI: Gale Group.
http://galenet.galegroup.com/servlet/HistRC
Document Number: CD2158000157

Document E

Letter from Impoverished Woman to Eleanor Roosevelt

Letter to Mrs. F.D. Roosevelt (1935)

Mrs. F.D. Roosevelt Washington D.C.

Chicago Ill 4/3-35

Dear Mrs. Roosevelt:--

Please pardon the liberty I am taking in writing you this note. Like thousands of others have lost and used up what we have saved, have been forced to go on relief. Have been compelled to store the small amt of things we had, and live in one room which is detrimental to our health, and unless we can raise our storage chg. Amt $28 by 4/10 the things may be sold for storage while not so valuable to any one else there are things that Cannot be replaced. I would like to borrow the amt $28 so I can pay the chg. and get a More healthful place to live. We are American born citizens and have always been self-supporting. It is very humiliating for me to have to write you Asking you again to pardon the privilege I am taking. I am hoping I may hear from you without publicity by ret. post.

Very Respectfully

Mrs.

Source Citation: Unknown. "Letter from Impoverished Woman to Eleanor Roosevelt." Reproduced in History Resource Center. Farmington Hills, MI: Gale Group.
http://galenet.galegroup.com/servlet/HistRC/
Document Number: CD2161000280

Document F

Letter to Eleanor Roosevelt Asking for Baby Clothes

Troy, N.Y. Jan. 2, 1935.

Dear Mrs. Roosevelt,

About a month ago I wrote you asking if you would buy some baby clothes for me with the understanding that I was to repay you as soon as my husband got enough work. Several weeks later I received a reply to apply to a Welfare Association so I might receive the aid I needed. Do you remember?

Please Mrs. Roosevelt, I do not want charity, only a chance from someone who will trust me until we can get enough money to repay the amount spent for the things I need. As a proof that I really am sincere. I am sending you two of my dearest possessions to keep as security, a ring my husband gave me before we were married, and a ring my mother used to wear. Perhaps the actual value of them is not high, but they are worth a lot to me. If you will consider buying the baby clothes, please keep them (rings) until I send you the money you spent. It is very hard to face bearing a baby we cannot afford to have, and the fact that it is due to arrive soon, and still there is no money for the hospital or clothing, does not make it any easier. I Have decided to stay home, keeping my 7 year old daughter from school to help with the smaller children when my husband has work. The oldest little girl is sick now, and has never been strong, so I would not depend on her. The 7 year old one is a good willing little worker and somehow we must manage--but without charity.

If you still feel you cannot trust me, it is allright and I can only say I do not blame you, but if you decide my word is worth anything with so small a security, here is a list of what I will need--but I will need it very soon.

2 shirts, silk and wool, size 23 pr. stockings, silk and wool, 4 1/2 or 43 straight flannel bands 2 slips--outing flannel 2 muslim dresses 1 sweater 1 wool bonnet 2 pr. wool booties 2 doz. diapers 30 x 30--or 27 x 27 1 large blanket (baby) about 45 (inches) or 50 (inches) 3 outing flannel nightgowns

If you will get these for me I would rather no one knew about it. I promise to repay the cost of the layette as soon as possible. We will all be very grateful to you, and I will be more than happy.

Sincerely yours,

Mrs. H. E. C.

Source Citation: H.E.C. (Mrs.). "Letter to Eleanor Roosevelt Asking for Baby Clothes." Reproduced in History Resource Center. Farmington Hills, MI: Gale Group.
http://galenet.galegroup.com/servlet/HistRC/
Document Number: CD2161000281

The Family of an Automobile Worker

A few months ago the Chevrolet plant in Atlanta was shut down and all the workers were idle for several weeks. But now the labor troubles are over, and the plant is working five days a week. The change in the outlook of the employee was typified in the expression of Mr. Whelchel when he came into the labor union office with a broad grin on his face, to get the lunch that his oldest son had brought in a basket. He recognized one of the interviewers, who had formerly taught a class among the automobile workers. They exchanged quick, hearty greetings before Mr. Whelchel hurried into the back of the office with his lunch. The interviewer asked if it would be all right for him to go down and interview his wife.

"Sure, go ahead."

The Whelchels live on a side street near the automobile plant, in a brown frame house of seven rooms - seven small rooms, as we found when we made a tour of the house. The lot is narrow but deep, stretching back almost two hundred feet to form a pasture for the cow which supplies the family with milk. The front yard is very small, but sodded with bermuda grass. The houses around the Whelchel's are similar in style and size, all frame structures, with small front yards planted in grass, and a few shrubs here and there.

Mrs. Whelchel was sitting on the porch, with her youngest child on her lap. She was combing and curling its hair. When we told her what we wanted she said that we had come to the wrong place, for she didn't think that she could tell us much that would be interesting. However, she began talking anyway, and told us that she was chairman of the home arts committee of the Women's Auxiliary. The home arts class, she said, was then working on some "gypsy glaze" pictures. She showed them to us later, and we found them to be designs painted on glass in transparent colors, with tinfoil on the back to reflect the light. She showed them with pride and sincere interest, and was genuinely pleased when we evidenced some enthusiasm over a design of a [sombre?] looking ship sailing a black ocean. She regarded her work critically, and remarked of one of the pictures, "I haven't ever been satisfied with the way that bird in the middle looks. I'll have to do it over." Impartially considered, the pictures were crude and gaudy, inharmonious mixtures of bright reds, yellows, and greens; but it was obvious that they were to Mrs. Whechel an outlet for the creative impulse. She did not draw the designs freehand, she said, but traced them from stencils the teacher of the class supplied. They included a ship, butterflies, and flowers, and parrots.

Source Citation: Unknown. "The Family of an Automobile Worker." Reproduced in History Resource Center. Farmington Hills, MI: Gale Group.
http://galenet.galegroup.com/servlet/HistRC/
Document Number: CD2158000045

People lined up for food at a New York City relief kitchen

Unemployed by the Great Depression, large numbers of people line up for food at a New York City relief kitchen.

AP/Wide World Photos. Reproduced by permission.

Source Citation: Reproduced in History Resource Center. Farmington Hills, MI: Gale Group.
http://galenet.galegroup.com/servlet/HistRC/
Document Number: CD2210040858

D-Day: The Story of the Allied Soldiers Who Invaded Europe

Sources from *History Resource Center: U.S.*

France Invaded by the Allies, June 6, 1944

Source Citation: "France Invaded by the Allies, June 6, 1944." DISCovering World History.
Gale Research, 1997. Reproduced in History Resource Center. Farmington Hills, MI: Gale Group.
http://galenet.galegroup.com/servlet/HistRC/
Document Number: BT2105241212

This essay identifies the major players and events leading to D-Day.

Normandy Invaded by the Allies, June 6, 1944

Source Citation: "Normandy Invaded, June 6, 1944." *DISCovering U.S. History.* Gale Research, 1997.
Reproduced in History Resource Center. Farmington Hills, MI: Gale Group.
http://galenet.galegroup.com/servlet/HistRC/
Document Number: BT2104241288

This overview of the Normandy invasion includes pictures.

Eisenhower as a Military Leader

Source Citation: "Dwight D. Eisenhower as a Military Leader." *History in Dispute, Vol. 4: World War II,
1939–1943.* Dennis Showalter, ed. St. James Press, 2000. Reproduced in History Resource Center.
Farmington Hills, MI: Gale Group.
http://galenet.galegroup.com/servlet/HistRC
Document Number: BT2306200118

This document summarizes two opposing views of Eisenhower's leadership of the Allied Expeditionary
Force in Western Europe.

General Eisenhower Meets with Troops on D-Day

Source Citation: Reproduced in History Resource Center. Farmington Hills, MI: Gale Group.
http://galenet.galegroup.com/servlet/HistRC
Document Number: BT2210018801

General Eisenhower gives the command, "Full victory—nothing else," to paratroopers on D-Day.

U.S. Soldiers landing at Normandy

Source Citation: Reproduced in History Resource Center. Farmington Hills, MI: Gale Group.
http://galenet.galegroup.com/servlet/HistRC
Document Number: BT2210011054

U.S. soldiers land on the beaches of Normandy under heavy Nazi machine-gun fire.

Overview

In 1940, Nazi Germany invaded France and took control of all Western Europe. The German leader, Adolf Hitler, claimed that his country would rule Europe for a thousand years. Hitler backed up his claim with one of the most powerful military forces ever assembled. The United States, Great Britain, the Soviet Union, and other countries opposed Hitler and the Germans. They formed an Allied army with the goal to defeat the Germans and free Europe from Nazi control.

To defeat the Germans, the Allies eventually would have to bring a large army into Europe. This wouldn't be easy, because the Germans created strong defenses all along the European coast where landings were possible. The coast was lined with barbed wire, mines, armed concrete bunkers, huge wooden posts rigged with explosives, and an underwater network of sharp steel barriers. These fortifications were known as the Atlantic Wall.

On February 12, 1944, General Dwight D. Eisenhower received a directive to begin planning Operation Overlord. Eisenhower knew that tens of thousands of soldiers would die in the invasion, but the war could not be won without landing soldiers in Europe. Eisenhower began planning the largest and most difficult wartime invasion in history. He chose the beaches of Normandy, France, for the invasion.

German military leaders knew the Allies were organizing an invasion of German-occupied France, but they did not know when or where it would occur. Rumor spread that the Allies would invade the French seaport of Calais. The Germans increased their forces at Calais, but they were still dug in strongly at Normandy.

Activities

Focus Activity: Simulation

You are an Allied officer who must tell your soldiers about the D-Day invasion. Prepare a five-minute briefing about the coming invasion. Your talk should be broken into two parts: The first part should inform the soldiers about the battle plans and what to expect from the German defenders. The second part of the briefing should talk about the personal dangers your soldiers will face and the bravery they will need in the battle.

Use the primary sources that follow to prepare your talk. For additional background information, search *History Resource Center: U.S.* using the keywords *Normandy invasion* or *D-Day*.

France Invaded by the Allies, June 6, 1944

Normandy Invaded by the Allies, June 6, 1944

U.S. Soldiers Landing at Normandy

Focus on Writing

Select one of these writing prompts to continue your investigation of the D-Day invasion. Keep in mind the characteristics of the writing mode you choose. Also keep in mind the basic rules of grammar, usage, and mechanics.

Narrative Writing: Write a short story about a fictional soldier during the D-Day invasion. Include details and events from the primary sources to make the story realistic. Tell about your character's fears and hopes.

Persuasive Writing: The soldiers of World War II have been called "the greatest generation." Write an essay agreeing or disagreeing with this label. Use information from the primary sources and from your background reading to support your position.

Extension

Look through *History Resource Center: U.S.* to locate additional sources that relate to the D-Day invasion. Think about the main topic of this lesson. Think about the sources already listed. This process will help you determine appropriate search words or phrases.

After you have compiled a list of sources, determine the best way to share your findings with your class. The types of sources you find may give you clues about the best method for sharing your findings.

Document-Based Essay Question (DBQ)

The following question requires you to construct a coherent essay that integrates your interpretation of Documents A–E and your knowledge of the period referred to in the question. Your essay should cite key pieces of evidence from the documents and draw on knowledge of Murrin, Chapter 26, "America during the Second World War."

Analyze Dwight D. Eisenhower's leadership during World War II. Was he a brilliant military leader or merely an effective coordinator during the retaking of Western Europe?

Use the documents and your knowledge of World War II to construct your essay.

Document A

France Invaded by the Allies, June 6, 1944

Principal Personages

Winston Leonard Spencer Churchill, Prime Minister of Great Britain

Franklin Roosevelt, thirty-second President of the United States

Joseph Stalin (Iosif Vissarionovich Dzhugashvili), Soviet Dictator

George Catlett Marshall, General, Chief of Staff United States Army

Dwight David Eisenhower, General, Supreme Commander Allied Expeditionary Force

Bernard Law Montgomery, General, Commander of the Allied Armies in northern France

Adolph Hitler, Chancellor and Führer of Germany

Karl Rudolf Gerd von Rundstedt, Field Marshal, German Commander-in-chief on the Western Front

Erwin Rommel, Field Marshal, German Commander of Army Group B and Inspector of Coastal Defenses

Summary of Event

After the German victory over France in 1940, one of the main objectives of the Allied powers was to invade France and inflict defeat upon Germany. Indeed, when the United States entered the European conflict in 1941, American generals proposed an immediate Anglo-American invasion of France as the first and most important step in defeating Germany. This proposal for an immediate invasion did not match British plans; the British Prime Minister, Winston Churchill, was afraid that an invasion with the limited resources then available would fail. He proposed instead that an attack upon German and Italian troops in the Mediterranean would offer greater advantages with fewer troops.

Franklin D. Roosevelt, the thirty-second President of the United States, together with General George C. Marshall, the Chief of Staff United States Army, continued to press for an invasion of France. So also did Joseph Stalin, the Soviet Dictator, who wanted a second front to take German pressure off the battlefields in Russia. A problem was lack of landing craft for such a large operation. The Americans had sufficient troops, but landing craft production was divided between the Pacific campaigns and the European ones, and it was not until 1944 that there were sufficient craft to support an invasion of France.

In 1943, planning for an invasion of France, named Operation Overlord, was put into full force. Anglo-American troops were to be shipped from the Mediterranean, where an invasion of Italy had already taken place, to a staging area in southern England. The invasion was scheduled to take place in May or June of 1944. General Dwight D. Eisenhower, the Commander of United States forces in Europe, was selected as Supreme Commander of the Allied Expeditionary Force, and Great Britain's General Bernard Law Montgomery, the hero of El Alamein, was appointed to command the Twenty-First Army Group, the main Allied land force. The beaches of Normandy were selected for the primary invasion. Eisenhower knew that the invasion would have to be successful on the first day; a beachhead had to be established, because with the scarcity of landing craft it would be six weeks before he would be able to land enough men to achieve numerical superiority over the German defenders. Thus, everything depended on the outcome of the first day's operations.

Document A

On the Continent, Adolf Hitler, the Chancellor and Führer of Germany, was aware of the fact that the Allies were planning an invasion, and since 1940, coastal defenses had been constructed in northern France. In 1944 he appointed Field Marshal Gerd von Rundstedt as German commander in the West, and Field Marshal Erwin Rommel as Commander of Army Group B, the main German army in northern France. He also made Rommel Inspector of Coastal Defenses. But Hitler retained personal command of the entire defense operation, so there was much overlapping of responsibility, and poor defense planning resulted.

Rundstedt contended that the Allies would be able to land anywhere along the coast, and therefore his best defense would be to hold the armor in reserve and send it to the battlefield when the Allies landed. But the Allies anticipated this strategy, and in the spring of 1944, they bombed communication and transportation lines along the entire coastal area to prevent the armor from moving fast enough to prevent the establishment of a beachhead. Rommel believed that, given the air situation, the best chance of defense lay in making a guess where the Allies would land and building up coastal defenses in that area; he, like Eisenhower, knew that all would be decided on the first day. Rommel chose the Pas de Calais area for his strong defense.

The Allies waited expectantly for the proper combination of tides and weather. Then, on June 6, 1944, the Allied invasion began. It was the largest combined air, sea, and land operation in history. After a day of bitter fighting the Allies established a beachhead in Normandy. Both Rommel and Hitler believed that the Normandy invasion was a feint for a larger invasion at Calais and kept troops away from Normandy. Rundstedt was unable to move his armor in time to stem the Allied troops.

Within a few days, the Allies broke through the Normandy defenses and were racing towards Paris. A massive battle against German armor at Caen held up Montgomery for a few days, but victory opened the way to Paris. Another Allied invasion of southern France took place in the middle of August and on August 25, 1944, Paris was liberated. The way was open to an invasion of Germany itself.

Source Citation: "France Invaded by the Allies, June 6, 1944." DISCovering World History. Gale Research, 1997. Reproduced in History Resource Center. Farmington Hills, MI: Gale Group.
http://galenet.galegroup.com/servlet/HistRC/
Document Number: BT2105241212

Eisenhower as a Military Leader

Viewpoint: Yes, Eisenhower was an effective military leader who brilliantly led the Allied Expeditionary Force to crush the Wehrmacht in western Europe.

General of the Army Dwight D. "Ike" Eisenhower emerged from World War II in resplendent glory. As Supreme Commander of the Allied Expeditionary Force, Eisenhower directed the vast array of Western armies that landed on **D-Day** (6 June 1944) and in the ensuing campaigns crushed the *Wehrmacht* (German Army) in the west. By Eisenhower's own account on the day of the surrender, there were more than three million Americans serving under his direct command. Combined forces led by Eisenhower on V-E Day (8 May 1945) exceeded four million combatants. He was by any standard one of the most successful coalition commanders in history.

Successful leadership in modern warfare is based on two fundamental principles: knowing what to do and knowing how to do it. A commander can learn the first tenet by schooling and experience. Comprehending the second principle is what marks a successful commander. The twenty-six years of Eisenhower's career prior to World War II witnessed the development of a highly adept professional officer. By taking advantage of the opportunities for formal military education, by learning the complexities and efficient operations of multi-echelon staffs and by studying under the tutelage of the army's most forward-looking officers, Eisenhower developed the techniques that prepared him for the awesome task confronting him. From 8 November 1942 until the ultimate defeat of Nazi Germany, Eisenhower commanded the most effective military coalition in history. He had no precedents on which to base his decisions. He faced innumerable obstacles, including the organization of a truly joint and combined allied staff.

Viewpoint: No, at best Eisenhower was an effective coordinator of Allied resources; he remained too removed from actual battle to be called a leader.

From the early years of World War II, Dwight D. Eisenhower's fitness to lead **Allied soldiers** became a controversial issue, and it remains so. Nationalism, service pride, and individual egos have influenced the international debate on Eisenhower's effectiveness as the strategic commander of Allied forces. When the war started in Europe in September 1939, Eisenhower was a lieutenant colonel with considerable staff and administrative experience, but little experience in leading soldiers and commanding tactical units. By 1944, as Commander of the Allied Expeditionary Forces, Eisenhower commanded and directed all Allied air, sea, and land forces in the Normandy invasion. He then planned and directed the northwest Europe theater strategy until the end of the war in May 1945. Eisenhower's rise from lieutenant colonel to general was nothing less than amazing. He achieved senior rank without commanding majortactical or operational units, and without service in combat. The question is: was Eisenhower an effective strategic commander, despite his lack of command experience at tactical and operational levels?

When Eisenhower was given command of the landings in North Africa in 1942, he had neither the experience nor the knowledge in operational and tactical doctrine to command such an operation. During the campaign Eisenhower's lack of experience was consistently obvious. As recorded by Martin Blumenson and James L. Stokesbury in *Masters of the Art of Command* (1975), the British Chief of the Imperial General Staff, Field Marshal Lord Alanbrooke, wrote that Eisenhower had neither the tactical nor strategical experience required for such a task.

Document B

By bringing Alexander over from the Middle East and appointing him as Deputy to Eisenhower, we were... flattering and pleasing the Americans in so far as we were placing our senior and experienced commander to function under their commander who had no war experience.

Source Citation: "Dwight D. Eisenhower as a Military Leader." *History in Dispute, Vol. 4: World War II, 1939–1943*. Dennis Showalter, ed. St. James Press, 2000. Reproduced in History Resource Center. Farmington Hills, MI: Gale Group. http://galenet.galegroup.com/servlet/HistRC
Document Number: BT2306200118

Document C

Normandy Invaded, June 6, 1944

Principal personages

DWIGHT DAVID EISENHOWER, GENERAL (1890–1969), Commander in Chief of Allied Forces in Western Europe

BERNARD LAW MONTGOMERY, GENERAL First Viscount Montgomery of Alamein (1887–1976), Commander Allied Armies in northern France

OMAR BRADLEY, GENERAL (1893–1981), Commander of the U.S. First Army

ERWIN ROMMEL, FIELD MARSHAL (1891–1944), Commander in charge of German defenses in Western Europe

KARL RUDOLF GERD VON RUNDSTEDT, FIELD MARSHAL (1875–1953), German Commander in Chief on the Western Front

ADOLF HITLER (1889–1945), Chancellor of Germany and Führer 1933–1945

Summary of Event

In January, 1944, General Dwight D. Eisenhower left the Mediterranean and came to England as Commander in Chief of Allied Forces in Western Europe to prepare the cross-Channel invasion. During the next five months, he directed the planning of the **operation** and the air offensive against the German defenses. The plans that British General Frederick Morgan had prepared for **"Overlord"** called for a three-division attack against Normandy. Eisenhower, along with his chief ground Commander, British General Bernard Law Montgomery, however, insisted on increasing the initial force to five divisions. Although most air force officers, both British and American, wanted to concentrate on a strategic bombing campaign inside Germany, Eisenhower ordered them to hit railroad centers, bridges, and other transportation targets inside France, in order to paralyze the German Army.

The attack had to begin at dawn, so that the troops would have a full day to drive inland and to establish a beachhead. Other requirements were a full moon the night before, so that parachute forces could be dropped; a low tide at dawn, so that the beach obstacles which

Document C

German Commander Erwin Rommel had erected could be cleared; and a fairly calm sea, since most of the Allied troops would cross the English Channel in small landing craft. The days of June 4, 5, and 6 would meet all the requirements assuming that the weather was good; the right combination of tide and moon would not occur again until mid-July. Eisenhower picked June 4 as D-Day.

Troop movements began on June 2, but the next day high winds made a landing on June 4 impossible. The adverse weather conditions continued the next day. That night, June 4, the weather prediction indicated that there would be a break in the storm and a period of relative calm beginning the night of June 5-6. Eisenhower held a council of war and decided to take the risk. On the morning of June 6 the weather did break, and more than five thousand Allied ships, carrying nearly 100,000 men, with 1,083 heavy bombers and more than two thousand fighter planes overhead, hit the beach. All the troops went ashore successfully, although the Americans at Omaha Beach could barely hold on to their position.

During the next week the Allied Expeditionary Force solidified its position. The Germans, because of the disruption of their transportation system and because of Allied air superiority, could not bring sufficient reserves to the battlefield to launch an effective counter-attack. They were strong enough, however, to seal off the beachhead. The British troops on Montgomery's left flank were unable to capture the city of Caen, a D-Day objective, until the middle of July; on the right flank, the U.S. First Army under General Omar Bradley captured the port of Cherbourg on June 27 but was unable to break out of the Cotentin Peninsula, where Field Marshal Erwin Rommel, in charge of German defenses, directed a skillful defense in the hedgerow country. Allied air power finally broke the deadlock. An intense bombardment on July 25 (4,200 tons of bombs saturated an area of only 2,500 by 6,000 yards) allowed General Bradley to break out. By August 1, his troops were in open country, and General George Patton's U.S. Third Army was sweeping forward through France. The German Seventh Army was partially destroyed and lost the bulk of its equipment at Falaise on August 13; on August 25, troops of the U.S. Third Army liberated Paris. British troops on the left joined the general advance, which by September 14 had carried the Allies to the Franco-German frontier and beyond Antwerp, Brussels, and Liege. The offensive then came to a halt, partly because the Germans succeeded in reëstablishing a defensive line but primarily because Eisenhower's men had outrun their supply lines and were short of equipment and matériel, especially gasoline for Patton's tanks. Montgomery criticized Eisenhower's strategy; the British officer argued that Eisenhower should have given all available supplies to the British troops on the left and allowed them to make a "single thrust" into Germany and Berlin, instead of spreading out his supplies on an equal basis among all the troops and advancing on a "broad front." Eisenhower contended that Montgomery's single thrust was risky and unworkable.

On December 16, Adolf Hitler, Führer of Germany, reinforced the troops on his Western Front by taking men from the Russian Front. He then ordered Field Marshal Karl von Rundstedt to launch a counterattack in the Ardennes region, aiming to split the American and British Armies and capture Antwerp. The offensive scored impressive gains on the first few days, but the Germans were not strong enough to sustain it. In the end, Hitler's Battle of the Bulge used up German strength and made a viable defense of the homeland impossible. The defeat of Nazi Germany had become imminent and inescapable.

Source Citation: **"Normandy Invaded, June 6, 1944."** *DISCovering U.S. History.* Gale Research, 1997. Reproduced in History Resource Center. Farmington Hills, MI: Gale Group.
http://galenet.galegroup.com/servlet/HistRC/
Document Number: BT2104241288

Document D

General Eisenhower gives the command,
"Full victory--nothing else," to paratroopers on D-day.

Courtesy of the National Archives

Source Citation: Reproduced in History Resource Center. Farmington Hills, MI: Gale Group.
http://galenet.galegroup.com/servlet/HistRC/
Document Number: BT2210018801

Document E

U.S. soldiers landing on the beaches of Normandy under heavy Nazi machine gun fire.

Courtesy of the National Archives

Source Citation: Reproduced in History Resource Center. Farmington Hills, MI: Gale Group.
http://galenet.galegroup.com/servlet/HistRC/
Document Number: BT2210011054

Politics at the End of the Twentieth Century: The Cold War Concludes

The Cold War, the Long Peace, and the Future

Source Citation: Gaddis, John Lewis. "The Cold War, the Long Peace, and the Future." Reproduced in History Resource Center. Farmington Hills, MI: Gale Group.
http://galenet.galegroup.com/servlet/HistRC/
Document Number: CD2165000079

This is a magazine article giving interpretations of the Cold War.

The Consequences of America's Cold War Policy

Source Citation: Pessen, Edward M. "The Consequences of America's Cold War Policy." Reproduced in History Resource Center. Farmington Hills, MI: Gale Group.
http://galenet.galegroup.com/servlet/HistRC/
Document Number: CD2165000173

This book offers interpretations of the Cold War.

An End to Which Cold War?

Source Citation: LaFeber, Walter. "An End to Which Cold War?" Reproduced in History Resource Center. Farmington Hills, MI: Gale Group.
http://galenet.galegroup.com/servlet/HistRC/
Document Number: CD2165000169

This is a magazine article giving interpretations of the Cold War.

Quiet Cataclysm: Some Afterthoughts about World War III

Source Citation: Mueller, John E. "Quiet Cataclysm: Some Afterthoughts about World War III." Reproduced in History Resource Center. Farmington Hills, MI: Gale Group.
http://galenet.galegroup.com/servlet/HistRC/
Document Number: CD2165000078

In this magazine article, a political scientist offers that the Cold War was primarily a war about ideas.

Victory in the Postwar Era: Despite the Cold War or Because of It?

Source Citation: Filitov, Alexei. "Victory in the Postwar Era: Despite the Cold War or Because of It?" Reproduced in History Resource Center. Farmington Hills, MI: Gale Group.
http://galenet.galegroup.com/servlet/HistRC/
Document Number: CD21650000577

In this magazine article, Alexei Filitov of the Institute of World History in Moscow adopted a different interpretation on the end of the Cold War from those that prevailed in the United States.

Some Lessons from the Cold War

Source Citation: Schlesinger, Arthur M., Jr. "Some Lessons from the Cold War." Reproduced in History Resource Center. Farmington Hills, MI: Gale Group.
http://galenet.galegroup.com/servlet/HistRC/
Document Number: CD2165000168

This is a magazine article by Arthur Schlesinger with interpretations of the Cold War.

Why Did the Cold War Arise, and Why Did It End?

Source Citation: Garthoff, Raymond L. "Why Did the Cold War Arise, and Why Did It End?" Reproduced in History Resource Center. Farmington Hills, MI: Gale Group.
http://galenet.galegroup.com/servlet/HistRC/
Document Numbeer: CD2165000080

This newspaper/magazine article, written in 1992, gives a perspective of the Cold War.

A Balance Sheet: Lippmann, Kennan, and the Cold War

Source Citation: Barnet, Richard J. "A Balance Sheet: Lippmann, Kennan, and the Cold War." Reproduced in History Resource Center. Farmington Hills, MI: Gale Group.
http://galenet.galegroup.com/servlet/HistRC/
Document Number: CD2165000081

This is a magazine article assessing the meaning and implications of the Cold War.

The End and the Beginning

Source Citation: Steel, Ronald. "The End and the Beginning." Reproduced in History Resource Center. Farmington Hills, MI: Gale Group.
http://galenet.galegroup.com/servlet/HistRC/
Document Number: CD2165000072

This is a magazine article providing interpretations of the Cold War.

The U.S. Government, a Legacy of the Cold War

Source Citation: May, Ernest R. "The U.S. Government, a Legacy of the Cold War." Reproduced in History Resource Center. Farmington Hills, MI: Gale Group.
http://galenet.galegroup.com/servlet/HistRC/
Document Number: CD2165000171

In this magazine article, a historian and leading expert on the foreign-policy bureaucracy traces the emergence of the U.S. "national-security state" during the Cold War and its implications for the post–Cold War era.

A View from Below

Source Citation: Chomsky, Noam. "A View from Below." Reproduced in History Resource Center. Farmington Hills, MI: Gale Group.
http://galenet.galegroup.com/servlet/HistRC/
Document Number: CD2165000170

This is a magazine article in which Noam Chomsky offers an interpretation of the Cold War.

Tumbling Down

Source Citation: Simpson, John. "Tumbling Down."
Reproduced in History Resource Center. Farmington Hills,
MI: Gale Group.
http://galenet.galegroup.com/servlet/HistRC/
Document Number: CD2165000075

In this book, a British journalist gives an eyewitness account
of the fall of the Berlin Wall.

German Hammers at Berlin Wall

Source Citation: Reproduced in History Resource Center.
Farmington Hills, MI: Gale Group.
http://galenet.galegroup.com/servlet/HistRC/
Document Number: CD2210036482

This is an image of Germans tearing the wall with hammers.

Mr. Gorbachev, Tear Down This Wall

Source Citation: Reproduced in History Resource
Center. Farmington Hills, MI: Gale Group.
http://galenet.galegroup.com/servlet/HistRC/
Document Numbeer: CD2210036481

Overview

"Cold War" is the term for the nonviolent but hostile relations that existed between the United Soviet Socialist Republic (USSR) and the United States from the end of World War II to 1991. This included an ongoing competition in the number and power of weapons possessed, known as an arms race. There are differences of opinion, however, as to exactly what and who brought about the end of the Cold War.

Some credit the end of the Cold War to President Ronald Reagan's (1981–1989) firm stance against the Soviet Union in the early 1980s. Reagan's position was that containment was no longer an option; the world could no longer coexist with communism. In March 1983, he announced plans for an increased military buildup by the United States. Reagan hoped that this buildup, known as "Star Wars," would put pressure on the Soviet Union and help them realize that they could never win a war with the U.S.

Others argue that the Soviet Union collapsed because of weaknesses within that country, primarily brought about by its mass military spending. When Mikhail Gorbachev became Soviet leader in 1985, he initiated several policies to reform the Soviet system. He realized that his country could no longer compete in the arms race and took a more conciliatory attitude toward the West. This led to an easing of tensions between the two countries. Gorbachev met with Reagan several times to discuss scaling back nuclear missiles. The Soviet Union pulled troops out of Afghanistan in 1989, and communist governments in several countries began to fall. The Berlin Wall, which had divided East and West Germany since 1961, was dismantled. The reforms that Gorbachev set into place backfired, and the USSR disintegrated in 1991.

Most do agree that the collapse of the USSR and, consequently, the end of the Cold War, was given a push by both Reagan and Gorbachev.

Focus Activity: Book Talk

Two people will present a book talk for television. One is an author of a book who offers unconventional assessments of the Cold War and disagrees that there was a "winner." The partner will have "read" the book and will ask questions about it. You will plan your book talk together so both will agree on the points made in the book. Your talk should be broken into two parts. The first part of the talk should give an overview of the Cold War. The second part of the talk should give the author's points.

Use the primary sources that follow to prepare your talk. For additional information, search *History Resource Center: U.S.* using the keywords *Cold War* and *postwar era*.

An End to Which Cold War?

The End and the Beginning

A View from Below

Focus on Writing

Select one of these writing prompts to continue your investigation of the end of the Cold War. Keep in mind the characteristics of the writing mode you choose. Also keep in mind the basic rules of grammar, usage, and mechanics.

Narrative Writing: You are in Berlin in 1989. Write a letter to your folks back home telling them about how it feels to see the wall come down. Use information from the primary sources and from your background reading to make the letter realistic.

Expository Writing: Compare assessments of the Cold War from these two sources: *A Balance Sheet: Lippmann, Kennan, and the Cold War* and *Victory in the Postwar Era: Despite the Cold War or Because of It?*

Extension

Look through *History Resource Center: U.S.* to locate additional sources that relate to the end of the Cold War. Think about the main topic of this lesson. Think about the sources already listed. This process will help you determine appropriate search words or phrases.

After you have compiled a list of sources, determine the best way to share your findings with your class. The types of sources you find may give you clues about the best method for sharing your findings.

Document-Based Essay Question (DBQ)

The following questions require you to construct a coherent essay that integrates your interpretation of Documents A–F and your knowledge of the period referred to in the questions. Your essay should cite key pieces of evidence from the documents and draw on knowledge of Murrin, Chapter 31, "Power and Politics since 1974."

Analyze the end of the Cold War. What brought about its end? What are some opposing viewpoints among historians, political scientists, and other experts about the Cold War and its ending?

Use the documents and your knowledge of the period of the early 1980s to 1991 to construct your essay.

Quiet Cataclysm: Some Afterthoughts about World War III

In the last few years we seem to have experienced something like the functional equivalent of World War III. The recent pleasantness (as Winston Churchill might have called it) was preceded, like its unpleasant and far noisier predecessors of 1914 and 1939, by a lengthy process in which rival countries jockeyed for position as they proclaimed competitive visions of the way the world ought to be ordered, armed themselves to the earlobes, made threatening noises, and confronted each other in traumatic crises. Like World Wars I and II, a consequence of the event was that a major empire was dismembered, important political boundaries in Europe were reorganized, and several nations were politically transformed. And, just as the ancient institution of monarchy met its effective demise in Europe in World War I and as the newer, but dangerous and seemingly virile ideologies of naziism and fascism were destroyed by World War II, so a major political philosophy, communism, over which a great deal of ink and blood had been spilled, was discredited and apparently expunged in World War III.

Source Citation: Mueller, John E. "Quiet Cataclysm: Some Afterthoughts about World War III." Reproduced in History Resource Center. Farmington Hills, MI: Gale Group.
http://galenet.galegroup.com/servlet/HistRC/
Document Number: CD2165000078

Some Lessons from the Cold War

In those faraway days when the Cold War was young, the English historian Sir Herbert Butterfield lectured at Notre Dame on "The Tragic Element in Modern International Conflict." Historians writing about modern wars, Butterfield said, characteristically start off with a "heroic" vision of things. They portray good men struggling against bad, virtue resisting evil. In this embattled mood, they see only the sins of the enemy and ignore the underlying structural dilemmas that so often provoke international clashes.

As time passes and emotions subside, history enters the "academic" phase. Now historians see "a terrible human predicament" at the heart of the story, "a certain situation that contains the element of conflict irrespective of any special wickedness in any of the parties concerned." Wickedness may deepen the predicament, but conflict would be there anyway. Perspective, Butterfield proposed, teaches us "to be a little more sorry for both parties than they knew how to be for one another." History moves on from melodrama to tragedy.

Source Citation: Schlesinger, Arthur M., Jr. "Some Lessons from the Cold War." Reproduced in History Resource Center. Farmington Hills, MI: Gale Group.
http://galenet.galegroup.com/servlet/HistRC/
Document Number: CD2165000168

Document C

Why Did the Cold War Arise, and Why Did It End?

The fundamental underlying cause of the Cold War was the reinforcing belief in both the Soviet Union and the United States that confrontation was unavoidable, imposed by history. Soviet leaders believed that communism would ultimately triumph in the world and that the Soviet Union was the vanguard Socialist/Communist state. They also believed that the Western "imperialist" powers were historically bound to pursue a hostile course against them. For their part, American and other Western leaders assumed that the Soviet Union was determined to enhance its own power and to pursue expansionist policies by all expedient means in order to achieve a Soviet-led Communist world. Each side thought that it was compelled by the very existence of the other side to engage in a zero-sum competition, and each saw the unfolding history of the Cold War as confirming its views.

The prevailing Western view was wrong in attributing a master plan to the Kremlin, in believing that Communist ideology impelled Soviet leaders to advance, in exaggerating Communist abilities to subvert the Free World, and in thinking that Soviet officials viewed military power as an ultimate recourse. But the West was not wrong in believing that Soviet leaders were committed to a historically driven struggle between two worlds until, ultimately, theirs would triumph. To be sure, other motivations, interests, and objectives played a part, including national aims, institutional interests, and personal psychological considerations. But these influences tended to enhance the ideological framework rather than weaken it. Moreover, the actions of each side were sufficiently consistent with the ideological expectations of the other side to sustain their respective worldviews for many years.

Source Citation: Garthoff, Raymond L. "Why Did the Cold War Arise, and Why Did It End?" Reproduced in History Resource Center. Farmington Hills, MI: Gale Group.
http://galenet.galegroup.com/servlet/HistRC/
Document Numbeer: CD2165000080

A Balance Sheet: Lippmann, Kennan, and the Cold War

Such reputations as present-day enjoy owe much to the fact that the newspaper columns they wrote forty-three days ago have already become recycled paper. Re-reading Walter Lippmann's columns on George Kennan's "X" article forty-three years after they were first published--in my case on the very day that the World War II conquerors relinquished their powers over Germany--is an unsettling experience. What are we to make of these twelve columns that Lippmann published a few months later as *The Cold War*? The clarity, the intellectual power, and the breadth of the analysis cannot fail to impress the reader, whatever one thinks of Lippmann's argument. As the United States stands on the threshold of another series of fateful choices, the contemporary relevance of the Lippmann-Kennan debate is striking.

The Cold War lays out a surprisingly coherent view of politics and diplomacy. It is a traditionalist, realist argument for a path not taken. Embedded in these columns and in Kennan's "Sources of Soviet Conduct" are many of the concerns that are likely to engage future historians of the Cold War. What was the Cold War? Was it inevitable? Could it have ended sooner? Is it reasonable to think that it could have ended differently under happier circumstances? (It is easy to imagine it ending under far worse.) What were the costs? Were any of them avoidable?

Source Citation: Barnet, Richard J. "A Balance Sheet: Lippmann, Kennan, and the Cold War." Reproduced in History Resource Center. Farmington Hills, MI: Gale Group.
http://galenet.galegroup.com/servlet/HistRC/
Document Number: CD2165000081

The End and the Beginning

During the darkest periods of the Cold War, parallels were sometimes drawn to World War I. Armed conflict, it was said, could break out, as it had in 1914, through miscalculation, rhetorical posturing, and the technological imperatives of the new weaponry. What was not imagined, however, was that the Cold War might suddenly come to an end in a way strikingly similar to that in which the war had ended on the eastern front in 1918: through the internal collapse and unconditional withdrawal of one of the belligerents. That one of the two superpowers might simply retire from the contest, that it would lose its empire and its internal cohesion, seemed no less improbable seventy-five years ago than, in a different context, does the demise of its successor today.

The collapse of the Russian state, which allowed the Bolsheviks to seize power, and the withdrawal of Russia from the war after the surrender at Brest-Litovsk, resulted from the rigidities of autocratic rule, the costs of fighting an interminable war, and the loss of faith by the nation's elite in the system itself. After the event, what had hitherto seemed unthinkable became strikingly obvious: Of course the Russian state, so outwardly formidable and unyielding, was merely a shell. Beneath the facade of invincibility, however, it was ripe for disintegration. It was almost inevitable, considering the toll of war, that the Romanov dynasty would fall. Was this not evident?

Source Citation: Steel, Ronald. "The End and the Beginning." Reproduced in History Resource Center. Farmington Hills, MI: Gale Group.
http://galenet.galegroup.com/servlet/HistRC/
Document Number: CD2165000072

Document F

Victory in the Postwar Era: Despite the Cold War or Because of It?

It is natural to analyze war in terms of victory and defeat, and so it is almost inevitable that the end of the Cold War will be analyzed in these terms. But is the concept of victory and defeat an appropriate analytical framework for understanding the outcome of the Cold War? What state can possibly claim victory in the Cold War--certainly not the Soviet Union. But can the United States be considered the victor either?

It seems unlikely that either superpower "won" the Cold War when one compares their relative positions in the world prior to the Cold War with their positions afterward. In 1945 the United States had a monopoly on atomic weapons and was virtually invulnerable to attack. By the end of the Cold War both superpowers had massive atomic arsenals and shared equal insecurity under the regime of Mutual Assured Destruction, a situation that left the Soviet Union no better off than before and that clearly marked a decline in American power.

Source Citation: Filitov, Alexei. "Victory in the Postwar Era: Despite the Cold War or Because of It?." Reproduced in History Resource Center. Farmington Hills, MI: Gale Group.
http://galenet.galegroup.com/servlet/HistRC/
Document Number: CD21650000577

Society and Culture at the End of the Twentieth Century: Immigration

Sources from *History Resource Center: U.S.*

Immigration Act of 1965

Source Citation: Congress, U.S. "Immigration Act of 1965." Reproduced in History Resource Center.
Farmington Hills, MI: Gale Group.
http://galenet.galegroup.com/servlet/HistRC/
Document Number: CD2154000069

This is legislation passed in October 1965 that was an amendment to the McCarran-Walter Act of 1952.

Remarks at the Signing of the Immigration Bill, 1965

Source Citation: Johnson, Lyndon B. "Remarks at the Signing of the Immigration Bill, 1965." Reproduced in History Resource Center. Farmington Hills, MI: Gale Group.
http://galenet.galegroup.com/servlet/HistRC/
Document Number: CD2154000111

This is a speech made by President Lyndon B. Johnson when he signed into law the Immigration Act of 1965.

Excerpt from Refugee Act of 1980

Source Citation: Congress, U.S. "Refugee Act of 1980." Reproduced in History Resource Center.
Farmington Hills, MI: Gale Group.
http://galenet.galegroup.com/servlet/HistRC/
Document Number: CD2154000114

This is legislation that established the principle of automatic admission to the United States for refugees with a "well-founded fear" of persecution because of "race, religion, nationality, membership in a particular social group, or political opinion."

An Act to Deter Immigration-Related Marriage Fraud

Source Citation: Congress, U.S. "An Act to Deter Immigration-Related Marriage Fraud." Reproduced in History Resource Center. Farmington Hills, MI: Gale Group.
http://galenet.galegroup.com/servlet/HistRC/
Document Number: CD2154000118

This is legislation that specifies that the participants to a marriage must remain married for two years in order for their union to be recognized as validating the immigrant's presence in the United States.

An Act to Revise and Reform Immigration Laws, 1986

Source Citation: Congress, U.S. "An Act to Revise and Reform Immigration Laws, 1986." Reproduced in History Resource Center. Farmington Hills, MI: Gale Group.
http://galenet.galegroup.com/servlet/HistRC/
Document Number: CD2154000119

This is legislation to reform immigration laws.

Beyond Disneyland

Source Citation: Lin, Mai. "Beyond Disneyland." Reproduced in History Resource Center. Farmington Hills, MI: Gale Group.
http://galenet.galegroup.com/servlet/HistRC/
Document Number: CD2157000072

This is an interview with the daughter of immigrants conducted in 1989, twelve years after the family emigrated from Taiwan to the United States.

Immigration Act

Source Citation: U.S. Congress. "Immigration Act." Reproduced in History Resource Center. Farmington Hills, MI: Gale Group.
http://galenet.galegroup.com/servlet/HistRC/
Document Number: CD2163000177

This is legislation passed in 1990 which, among other things, revised policy on legal immigration.

Will the Melting Pot Boil Over?

Source Citation: Ciria-Cruz, Rene P. "Will the Melting Pot Boil Over?" Reproduced in History Resource Center. Farmington Hills, MI: Gale Group.
http://galenet.galegroup.com/servlet/HistRC/
Document Number: CD2157000101

This is a magazine article from *Filipinas* magazine of August 1994.

Proposition 187

Source Citation: Unknown. "Proposition 187." Reproduced in History Resource Center. Farmington Hills, MI: Gale Group.
http://galenet.galegroup.com/servlet/HistRC/
Document Number: CD2154000115

This is a state provision passed in California that barred undocumented immigrants from receiving many social services that strained the state budget.

Excerpts of Report on U.S. Immigration Policy

Source Citation: Commission on Immigration Reform, U.S. "Excerpts of Report on U.S. Immigration Policy." Reproduced in History Resource Center. Farmington Hills, MI: Gale Group.
http://galenet.galegroup.com/servlet/HistRC/
Document Number: CD2154000116

This is a report issued by the United States Commission on Immigration to summarize the current status of immigration policy and to offer recommendations for reform.

Human Rights Watch Blasts INS Detention

Source Citation: Immigration News Briefs. "Human Rights Watch Blasts INS Detention." Reproduced in History Resource Center. Farmington Hills, MI: Gale Group.
http://galenet.galegroup.com/servlet/HistRC/
Document Number: CD2163000178

This is a newspaper/magazine article about accusations by the Human Rights Watch organization of abuses to illegal immigrants by the federal Immigration and Naturalization Service (INS).

Statement on Pending Immigration Reform Statute

Source Citation: Leadership Conference on Civil Rights. "Statement on Pending Immigration Reform Statute." Reproduced in History Resource Center. Farmington Hills, MI: Gale Group.
http://galenet.galegroup.com/servlet/HistRC/
Document Number: CD2163000182

This is a miscellaneous document of a statement by the Leadership Conference on Civil Rights in response to the proposed Illegal Immigration and Responsibility Act (1996).

Overview

The Immigration Act of 1965 eased restrictions and allowed increased numbers of immigrants into the United States. President John F. Kennedy initiated immigration reform, and President Lyndon Johnson signed the Immigration Act Amendments of 1965 into law.

The Immigration and Nationality Act of 1952, known as the McCarran-Walker Act, was in force until the Immigration Act Amendments of 1965. Criticism had arisen during the 1950s of the harshness of McCarran-Walker, particularly toward Asians. In addition, the civil-rights revolution in the 1960s led to less discriminatory attitudes toward immigration. Among other things, the amendments of 1965 increased the number of visas for people from the Eastern Hemisphere and allowed spouses; minor, unmarried children; and parents of U.S. citizens into the country regardless of quotas.

Proponents of the amendments, however, did not anticipate the concerns that would arise: questions related to refugees, illegal immigrants, and maintaining the flow of legal immigration. Domestic problems in Asia and Latin America caused an influx of people seeking employment. Over one million Filipinos came to the U.S. between 1971 and 1994 under the family reunification provisions. The U.S. recruited doctors and nurses between 1965 and 1974, and many Asian professionals took advantage of this effort. Other professionals from Korea and India

LBJ Library photo by Yoichi R. Okamoto

In 1965 President Lyndon Johnson repealed the McCarran-Walter Act, replacing national origins quotas with an annual allowance of 20,000 immigrants from each country.

Source Citation: Reproduced in History Resource Center. Farmington Hills, MI: Gale Group.
http://galenet.galegroup.com/servlet/HistRC/
Document Number: BT2210018613

entered under the occupational criteria of the amendments. More than half the entries from Latin American between 1971 and 1994 were from Mexico. Refugees also came after 1965. Cubans alone constituted 530,000 immigrants between 1961–1994. Others came from the Soviet Union. After Saigon fell in 1975, more than 585,000 Vietnamese immigrated to the U.S. along with numbers of Laotians and Cambodians.

In the 1970s, people began to be concerned about the large numbers of undocumented immigrants, primarily from the southern boundary, and immigration legislation by Congress increased after 1980. The Refugee Act of 1980 allowed people with well-founded fears of persecution to have automatic admission to the U.S.; the Immigration Reform and Control Act of 1986 set guidelines for controlling immigration, especially illegal immigration; the Immigration Marriage Fraud Amendments of 1986 addressed marriages made for purposes of citizenship; and the Immigration Act of 1990 revised policy on legal immigration, increased total admissions, and added diversity to those admissions.

Washington continues to be focused on immigration. Concerns about social services for undocumented immigrants have prompted attempts at reform, such as California's Proposition 187. Current immigration policies have led to political reactions against multiculturalism, such as calls to make English the official language of the United States. No one knows the future, but since 1965, the issue of controlling immigration has become a divisive one in the United States.

Activities

Focus Activity: Visuals

Create a visual that illustrates immigration in the United States from the Immigration Act of 1965 to the end of the twentieth century. Present your visual to the class in five minutes or less.

Use the primary sources that follow to prepare your visual. For additional information, search *History Resource Center: U.S.* using the keywords *immigration* and *immigration policy*.

Immigration Act of 1965

Excerpts of Report on U.S. Immigration Policy

Statement on Pending Immigration Reform Statute

Focus on Writing

Select one of these writing prompts to continue your investigation of immigration from 1965 to 1999. Keep in mind the characteristics of the writing mode you choose. Also keep in mind the basic rules of grammar, usage, and mechanics.

Narrative Writing: You are a high school student whose family has just immigrated to the United States. It is your first day at school. Write a letter to a friend back home telling what your day is like. Use information from the primary sources and from your background reading to make the letter realistic.

Expository Writing: Proponents of Proposition 187 took their fight to the national level. Write an essay agreeing or disagreeing with a national proposition similar to California Proposition 187. Use information from the primary sources and from your background reading to support your position.

Extension

Look through *History Resource Center: U.S.* to locate additional sources that relate to immigration after 1965. Think about the main topic of this lesson. Think about the sources already listed. This process will help you determine appropriate search words or phrases.

After you have compiled a list of sources, determine the best way to share your findings with your class. The types of sources you find may give you clues about the best method for sharing your findings.

Document-Based Essay Question (DBQ)

The following questions require you to construct a coherent essay that integrates your interpretation of Documents A–H and your knowledge of the period referred to in the questions. Your essay should cite key pieces of evidence from the documents and draw on knowledge of Murrin, Chapter 30, "Economic and Social Change in the Late 20th Century" and Chapter 31, "Power and Politics since 1974."

Analyze immigration in the United States from 1965 until the end of the twentieth century. How did the Immigration Act of 1965 contribute to demographic changes? What concerns arose after 1970 regarding immigration? How is immigration policy since 1965 connected to the civil-rights revolution of the 1960s?

Use the documents and your knowledge of the period of 1965–1999 to construct your essay.

Document A

Immigration Act, 1965

An Act To amend the Immigration and Nationality Act, and for other purposes.

Be it enacted by the Senate and House of Representatives of the United States of America in Congress assembled, That section 201 of the Immigration and Nationality Act (66 Stat. 175; 8 U.S.C. 1151) be amended to read as follows:

"Sec. 201. (a) Exclusive of special immigrants defined in section 101(a)(27), and of the immediate relatives of United States citizens specified in subsection (b) of this section, the number of aliens who may be issued immigrant visas or who may otherwise acquire the status of an alien lawfully admitted to the United States for permanent residence, or who may, pursuant to section 203(a)(7) enter conditionally, (i) shall not in any of the first three quarters of any fiscal year exceed a total of 45,000 and (ii) shall not in any fiscal year exceed a total of 170,000.

"(b) The `immediate relatives' referred to in subsection (a) of this section shall mean the children, spouses, and parents of a citizen of the United States: *Provided,* That in the case of parents, such citizen must be at least twenty-one years of age. The immediate relatives specified in this subsection who are otherwise qualified for admission as immigrants shall be admitted as such, without regard to the numerical limitations in this Act.

"(c) During the period from July 1, 1965, through June 30, 1968, the annual quota of any quota area shall be the same as that which existed for that area on June 30, 1965. The Secretary of State shall, not later than on the sixtieth day immediately following the date of enactment of this subsection and again on or before September 1, 1966, and September 1, 1967, determine and proclaim the amount of quota numbers which remain unused at the end of the fiscal year ending on June 30, 1965, June 30, 1966, and June 30, 1967, respectively, and are available for distribution pursuant to subsection (d) of this section.

"(d) Quota numbers not issued or otherwise used during the previous fiscal year, as determined in accordance with subsection (c) hereof, shall be transferred to an immigration pool. Allocation of numbers from the pool and from national quotas shall not together exceed in any fiscal year the numerical limitations in subsection (a) of this section. The immigration pool shall be made available to immigrants otherwise admissible under the provisions of this Act who are unable to obtain prompt issuance of a preference visa due to oversubscription of their quotas, or subquotas as determined by the Secretary of State. Visas and conditional entries shall be allocated from the immigration pool within the percentage limitations and in the order of priority specified in section 203 without regard to the quota to which the alien is chargeable.

"(e) The immigration pool and the quotas of quota areas shall terminate June 30, 1968. Thereafter immigrants admissible under the provisions of this Act who are subject to the numerical limitations of subsection (a) of this section shall be admitted in accordance with the percentage limitations and in the order of priority specified in section 203."

Source Citation: Congress, U.S. "Immigration Act of 1965." Reproduced in History Resource Center. Farmington Hills, MI: Gale Group.
http://galenet.galegroup.com/servlet/HistRC/
Document Number: CD2154000069

Document B

Excerpt of the Refugee Act, 1980

Title I--Purpose

Section 101. (a) The Congress declares that it is the historic policy of the United States to respond to the urgent needs of persons subject to persecution in their homelands, including, where appropriate, humanitarian assistance for their care and maintenance in asylum areas, efforts to promote opportunities for resettlement or voluntary repatriation, aid for necessary transportation and processing, admission to this country of refugees of special humanitarian concern to the United States, and transitional assistance to refugees in the United States. The Congress further declares that it is the policy of the United States to encourage all nations to provide assistance and resettlement opportunities to refugees to the fullest extent possible.

(b) The objectives of this Act are to provide a permanent and systematic procedure for the admission to this country of refugees of special humanitarian concern to the United States, and to provide comprehensive and uniform provisions for the effective resettlement and absorption of those refugees who are admitted.

Title II--Admission of Refugees

Section 201. (a) Section 101(a) of the Immigration and Nationality Act (8 U.S.C. 1101(a)) is amended by adding after paragraph (41) the following new paragraph:

"(42) The term 'refugee' means (A) any person who is outside any country of such person's nationality or, in the case of a person having no nationality, is outside any country in which such person last habitually resided, and who is unable or unwilling to return to, and is unable or unwilling to avail himself or herself of the protection of, that country because of persecution or a well-founded fear of persecution on account of race, religion, nationality, membership in a particular social group, or political opinion, or (B) in such special circumstances as the President after appropriate consultation (as defined in section 207(e) of this Act) may specify, any person who is within the country of such person's nationality or, in the case of a person having no nationality, within the country in which such person is habitually residing, and who is persecuted or who has a well-founded fear of persecution on account of race, religion, nationality, membership in a particular social group, or political opinion. The term 'refugee' does not include any person who ordered, incited, assisted, or otherwise participated in the persecution of any person on account of race, religion, nationality, membership in a particular social group, or political opinion."

(b) Chapter 1 of title II of such Act is amended by adding after section 206(8 U.S.C. 1156) the following new sections:

Annual Admission of Refugees and Admission of Emergency Situation Refugees

Section 207. (a)(1) Except as provided in subsection (b), the number of refugees who may be admitted under this section in fiscal year 1980, 1981, or 1982, may not exceed fifty thousand unless the President determines, before the beginning of the fiscal year and after appropriate consultation (as defined in subsection (e)), that admission of a specific number of refugees in excess of such number is justified by humanitarian concerns or is otherwise in the national interest.

"(2) Except as provided in subsection (b), the number of refugees who may be admitted under this section in any fiscal year after fiscal year 1982 shall be such number as the President determines, before the beginning of the fiscal year and after appropriate consultation, is justified by humanitarian concerns or is otherwise in the national interest.

Document B

"(3) Admissions under this subsection shall be allocated among refugees of special humanitarian concern to the United States in accordance with a determination made by the President after appropriate consultation.

"(b) If the President determines, after appropriate consultation, that (1) an unforeseen emergency refugee situation exists, (2) the admission of certain refugees in response to the emergency refugee situation is justified by grave humanitarian concerns or is otherwise in the national interest, and (3) the admission to the United States of these refugees cannot be accomplished under subsection (a), the President may fix a number of refugees to be admitted to the United States during the succeeding period (not to exceed twelve months) in response to the emergency refugee situation and such admissions shall be allocated among refugees of special humanitarian concern to the United States in accordance with a determination made by the President after the appropriate consultation provided under this subsection.

"(c)(1) Subject to the numerical limitations established pursuant to subsections (a) and (b), the Attorney General may, in the Attorney General's discretion and pursuant to such regulations as the Attorney General may prescribe, admit any refugee who is not firmly resettled in any foreign country, is determined to be of special humanitarian concern to the United States, and is admissible (except as otherwise provided under paragraph (3)) as an immigrant under this Act.

"(2) A spouse or child (as defined in section 101(b)(1)(A), (B), (C), (D), or (E)) of any refugee who qualifies for admission under paragraph (1) shall, if not otherwise entitled to admission under paragraph (1) and if not a person described in the second sentence of section 101(a)(42), be entitled to the same admission status as such refugee if accompanying, or following to join, such refugee and if the spouse or child is admissible (except as otherwise provided under paragraph (3)) as an immigrant under this Act. Upon the spouse's or child's admission to the United States, such admission shall be charged against the numerical limitation established in accordance with the appropriate subsection under which the refugee's admission is charged.

"(3) The provisions of paragraphs (14), (15), (20), (21), (25), and (32) of section 212(a) shall not be applicable to any alien seeking admission to the United States under this subsection, and the Attorney General may waive any other provision of such section (other than paragraph (27), (29), or (33) and other than so much of paragraph (23) as relates to trafficking in narcotics) with respect to such an alien for humanitarian purposes, to assure family unity, or when it is otherwise in the public interest. Any such waiver by the Attorney General shall be in writing and shall be granted only on an individual basis following an investigation. The Attorney General shall provide for the annual reporting to Congress of the number of waivers granted under this paragraph in the previous fiscal year and a summary of the reasons for granting such waivers.

Source Citation: Congress, U.S. "Refugee Act of 1980." Reproduced in History Resource Center. Farmington Hills, MI: Gale Group.
http://galenet.galegroup.com/servlet/HistRC/
Document Number: CD2154000114

An Act to Deter Immigration-Related Marriage Fraud

An Act to Deter Immigration-Related Marriage Fraud and Other Immigration Fraud

Public Law 99-63999th Congress

Be it enacted by the Senate and House of Representatives of the United States of America in Congress assembled,

SECTION 1. SHORT TITLE.

This Act may be cited as the "Immigration Marriage Fraud Amendments of 1986".

SEC. 2. DETERRING IMMIGRATION-RELATED MARRIAGE FRAUD.

(a) Conditional Basis for Permanent Resident Status Based on Recent Marriage. – Chapter 2 of title II of the Immigration and Nationality Act is amended by adding at the end the following new section:

"CONDITIONAL PERMANENT RESIDENT STATUS FOR CERTAIN ALIEN SPOUSES AND SONS AND DAUGHTERS

"Sec. 216. (a) In General.--

"(1) Conditional Basis For Status.--Notwithstanding any other provision of this Act, an alien spouse (as defined in subsection (g)(1)) and an alien son or daughter (as defined in subsection (g)(2)) shall be considered, at the time of obtaining the status of an alien lawfully admitted for permanent residence, to have obtained such status on a conditional basis subject to the provisions of this section.

"(2) Notice of Requirements.--

"(A) At time of obtaining permanent residence.--At the time an alien spouse or alien son or daughter obtains permanent resident status on a conditional basis under paragraph (1), the Attorney General shall provide for notice to such a spouse, son, or daughter respecting the provisions of this section and the requirements of subsection (c)(1) to have the conditional basis of such status removed.

"(B) At time of required petition.--In addition, the Attorney General shall attempt to provide notice to such a spouse, son, or daughter, at or about the beginning of the 90-day period described in subsection (d)(2)(A), of the requirements of subsections (c)(1).

"(C) Effect of failure to provide notice.--The failure of the Attorney General to provide a notice under this paragraph shall not affect the enforcement of the provisions of this section with respect to such a spouse, son, or daughter.

"(b) Termination of Status if Finding that Qualifying Marriage Improper.--

"(1) In general.--In the case of an alien with permanent resident status on a conditional basis under subsection (a), if the Attorney General determines, before the second anniversary of the alien's obtaining the status of lawful admission for permanent residence, that--

"(A) the qualifying marriage--

"(I) was entered into for the purpose of procuring an alien's entry as an immigrant, or

"(ii) has been judicially annulled or terminated, other than through the death of a spouse; or

"(B) a fee or other consideration was given (other than a fee or other consideration to an attorney for assistance in preparation of a lawful petition) for the filing of a petition under

Document C

section 204(a) or 214(d) with respect to the alien; the Attorney General shall so notify the parties involved and, subject to paragraph (2), shall terminate the permanent resident status of the alien (or aliens) involved as of the date of the determination.

"(2) Hearing in deportation proceeding.--Any alien whose permanent resident status is terminated under paragraph (1) may request a review of such determination in a proceeding to deport the alien. In such proceeding, the burden of proof shall be on the Attorney General to establish, by a preponderance of the evidence, that a condition described in paragraph (1) is met.

Source Citation: Congress, U.S. "An Act to Deter Immigration-Related Marriage Fraud." Reproduced in History Resource Center. Farmington Hills, MI: Gale Group.
http://galenet.galegroup.com/servlet/HistRC/
Document Number: CD2154000118

Document D

An Act to Revise and Reform the Immigration Laws, and Other Purposes

Public Law 99-60399th Congress

Be it enacted by the Senate and House of Representatives of the United States of America in Congress assembled,

SECTION 1. SHORT TITLE; REFERENCES IN ACT.

(a) **Short Title.**--This Act may be cited as the "Immigration Reform and Control Act of 1986".

(b) **Amendment to Immigration and Nationality Act.**--Except as otherwise specifically provided in this Act, whenever in this Act an amendment or repeal is expressed as an amendment to, or repeal of, a provision, the reference shall be deemed to be made to the Immigration and Nationality Act.

TABLE OF CONTENTS

Sec. 1. Short title; references in Act.

TITLE I--CONTROL OF ILLEGAL IMMIGRATION

Part A--Employment

Sec. 101. Control of unlawful employment of aliens.

Sec. 102. Unfair immigration-related employment practices.

Sec. 103. Fraud and misuse of certain immigration-related documents.

Part B--Improvement of Enforcement and Services

Sec. 111. Authorization of appropriations for enforcement and service activities of the Immigration and Naturalization Service.

Sec. 112. Unlawful transportation of aliens to the United States.

Sec. 113. Immigration emergency fund.

Sec. 114. Liability of owners and operators of international bridges and toll roads to prevent the unauthorized landing of aliens.

Sec. 115. Enforcement of the immigration laws of the United States.

Sec. 116. Restricting warrantless entry in the case of outdoor agricultural operations.

Sec. 117. Restrictions on adjustment of status.

Part C--Verification of Status Under Certain Programs

Sec. 121. Verification of immigration status of aliens applying for benefits under certain programs.

TITLE II--LEGALIZATION

Sec. 201. Legalization of status.

Sec. 202. Cuban-Haitian adjustment.

Sec. 203. Updating registry date to January 1, 1972.

Sec. 204. State legalization impact-assistance grants.

Source Citation: Congress, U.S. "An Act to Revise and Reform Immigration Laws, 1986." Reproduced in History Resource Center. Farmington Hills, MI: Gale Group.
http://galenet.galegroup.com/servlet/HistRC/
Document Number: CD2154000119

Immigration Reform and Control Act, 19908 USC Sec. 1227

TITLE 8 - ALIENS AND NATIONALITY CHAPTER 12 - IMMIGRATION AND NATIONALITY

SUBCHAPTER II - IMMIGRATION

Part IV - Inspection, Apprehension, Examination, Exclusion, and Removal

-HEAD- Sec. 1227. Deportable aliens

-STATUTE- (a) Classes of deportable aliens

Any alien (including an alien crewman) in and admitted to the United States shall, upon the order of the Attorney General, be removed if the alien is within one or more of the following classes of deportable aliens:

(1) Inadmissible at time of entry or of adjustment of status or violates status

(A) Inadmissible aliens any alien who at the time of entry or adjustment of status was within one or more of the classes of aliens inadmissible by the law existing at such time is deportable.

(B) Present in violation of law any alien who is present in the United States in violation of this chapter or any other law of the United States is deportable.

(C) Violated nonimmigrant status or condition of entry

(i) Nonimmigrant status violators any alien who was admitted as a nonimmigrant and who has failed to maintain the nonimmigrant status in which the alien was admitted or to which it was changed under section 1258 of this title, or to comply with the conditions of any such status, is deportable.

(ii) Violators of conditions of entry any alien whom the Secretary of Health and Human Services certifies has failed to comply with terms, conditions, and controls that were imposed under section 1182(g) of this title is deportable.

(D) Termination of conditional permanent residence

(i) In general Any alien with permanent resident status on a conditional basis under section 1186a of this title (relating to conditional permanent resident status for certain alien spouses and sons and daughters) or under section 1186b of this title (relating to conditional permanent resident status for certain alien entrepreneurs, spouses, and children) who has had such status terminated under such respective section is deportable.

(ii) Exception

Clause (i) shall not apply in the cases described in section 1186a(c)(4) of this title (relating to certain hardship waivers).

(E) Smuggling

(i) In general Any alien who (prior to the date of entry, at the time of any entry, or within 5 years of the date of any entry) knowingly has encouraged, induced, assisted, abetted, or aided any other alien to enter or to try to enter the United States in violation of law is deportable.

(ii) Special rule in the case of family reunification Clause (i) shall not apply in the case of alien who is an eligible immigrant (as defined in section 301(b)(1) of the Immigration Act of 1990), was physically present in the United States on May 5, 1988, and is seeking admission as an immediate relative or under section 1153(a)(2) of this title (including under section 112 of the

Immigration Act of 1990) or benefits under section 301(a) of the Immigration Act of 1990 if the alien, before May 5, 1988, has encouraged, induced, assisted, abetted, or aided only the alien's spouse, parent, son, or daughter (and no other individual) to enter the United States in violation of law.

(iii) Waiver authorized The Attorney General may, in his discretion for humanitarian purposes, to assure family unity, or when it is otherwise in the public interest, waive application of clause

(iv) In the case of any alien lawfully admitted for permanent residence if the alien has encouraged, induced, assisted, abetted, or aided only an individual who at the time of the offense was the alien's spouse, parent, son, or daughter (and no other individual) to enter the United States in violation of law.

(F) Repealed. Pub. L. 104-208, div. C, title VI, Sec. 671(d)(1)(C), Sept. 30, 1996, 110 Stat. 3009-723

Document F

U.S. Immigration Policy: Restoring Credibility

Introduction

The U.S. Commission on Immigration Reform was created by Congress to assess U.S. immigration policy and make recommendations regarding its implementation and effects. Mandated in the Immigration Act of 1990 to submit an interim report in 1994 and a final report in 1997, the Commission has undertaken public hearings, fact-finding missions, and expert consultations to identify the major immigration-related issues facing the United States today.

This process has been a complex one. Distinguishing fact from fiction has been difficult, in some cases because of what has become a highly emotional debate on immigration. We have heard contradictory testimony, shaky statistics, and a great deal of honest confusion regarding the impacts of immigration. Nevertheless, we have tried throughout to engage in what we believe is a systematic, non-partisan effort to reach conclusions drawn from analysis of the best data available.

Underlying Principles

Certain basic principles underlie the Commission's work. The Commission decries hostility and discrimination against immigrants as antithetical to the traditions and interests of the country. At the same time, we disagree with those who would label efforts to control immigration as being inherently anti-immigrant. Rather, it is both a right and a responsibility of a democratic society to manage immigration so that it serves the national interest.

Challenges Ahead

The Commission believes that legal immigration has strengthened and can continue to strengthen this country. While we will be reporting at a later date on the impacts of our legal immigration system, and while there may even be disagreements among us as to the total number of immigrants that can be absorbed into the United States or the categories that should be given priority for admission, the Commission members agree that immigration presents many opportunities for this nation. Immigrants can contribute to the building of the country. In most cases, they have been actively sought by family members or businesses in the U.S. The tradition of welcoming newcomers has become an important element of how we define ourselves as a nation.

The Commission is mindful of the problems that also emanate from immigration. In particular, we believe that unlawful immigration is unacceptable. Enforcement efforts have not been effective in deterring unlawful immigration. This failure to develop effective strategies to control unlawful immigration has blurred the public perception of the distinction between legal and illegal immigrants.

For the Commission, the principal issue at present is how to manage immigration so that it will continue to be in the national interest.

• How do we ensure that immigration is based on and supports broad national economic, social, and humanitarian interests, rather than the interests of those who would abuse our laws?

• How do we gain effective control over our borders while still encouraging international trade, investment, and tourism?

• How do we maintain a civic culture based on shared values while accommodating the large and diverse population admitted through immigration policy?

The credibility of immigration policy can be measured by a simple yardstick: people who should get in, do get in; people who should not get in are kept out; and people who are judged deportable are required to leave.

During the decade from 1980 to 1990, three major pieces of legislation were adopted to govern immigration policy--the Refugee Act of 1980, the Immigration Reform and Control Act of 1986, and the Immigration Act of 1990. The Commission supports the broad framework for immigration policy that these laws represent: a legal immigration system that strives to serve the national interest in helping families to reunify and employers to obtain skills not available in the U.S. labor force; a refugee system that reflects both our humanitarian beliefs and international refugee law; and an enforcement system that seeks to deter unlawful immigration through employer sanctions and tighter border control.

The Commission has concluded, however, that more needs to be done to guarantee that the stated goals of our immigration policy are met. The immediate need is more effective prevention and deterrence of unlawful immigration. This report to Congress outlines the Commission's recommendations in this area.

In the long term, immigration policies for the 1990s and beyond should anticipate the challenges of the next century. These challenges will be substantially influenced by factors such as the restructuring of our own economy, the establishment of such new trade relationships as the North American Free Trade Agreement [NAFTA], and changing geopolitical relations. No less importantly, immigration policy must carefully take into account social concerns, demographic trends, and the impact of added population on the country's environment.

Finally, current immigration is the first to occur in what economists call a post-industrial economy, just as it is the first to occur after the appearance of the modem welfare state. The Commission's report to Congress in 1997 will cover these issues in assessing the impact of the Immigration Act of 1990. The present report reviews the progress of the beginning implementation of this legislation.

Source Citation: Commission on Immigration Reform, U.S. "Excerpts of Report on U.S. Immigration Policy." Reproduced in History Resource Center. Farmington Hills, MI: Gale Group.
http://galenet.galegroup.com/servlet/HistRC/
Document Number: CD2154000116

STATEMENT OF THE LEADERSHIP CONFERENCE ON CIVIL RIGHTS on PENDING IMMIGRATION REFORM LEGISLATION

The Leadership Conference on Civil Rights is very concerned about the intent and effect of major provisions of the immigration bills currently pending in the House and Senate. The Leadership Conference is the nation's oldest, largest, and most broadly-based civil rights coalition, comprised of 180 national organizations representing racial and ethnic minorities, women, persons with disabilities, older Americans, labor, gays and lesbians, and major religious groups. The Leadership Conference has worked since its inception for equal opportunity and social justice for all individuals.

Review and evaluation of U.S. immigration laws and their implementation is always appropriate. The present debate, however, is being driven by negative politics and is dominated by distortion and hyperbole. Current proposals for comprehensive immigration reform (S. 269 and S. 1394, introduced by Senator Alan Simpson, and H.R. 2202, introduced by Rep. Lamar Smith) exploit poorly-informed public concern over undocumented immigration to impose unneeded and unwarranted reductions and restrictions on legal family-based immigration and on the rights of citizens and legal permanent residents.

1. Family immigration is not a problem and should be left alone

Both the House and the Senate bills unfairly capitalize on public concern about illegal immigration in order to substantially reduce the number of people coming to the United States as relatives of U.S. citizens and legal permanent residents. The effects of these reductions would fall most heavily on U.S. citizens -- most of whom are Latino and Asian in origin -- who wish to reunite with their closest family members. These communities rightfully point out that the changes being proposed are the most restrictive reforms to the immigration system since the 1924 National Origins Act, which is widely recognized as having been designed in order to pursue what was then perceived as desirable racial homogeneity.

The most drastic cuts in both the House and Senate bills would effectively eliminate immigration of adult children and brothers and sisters of U.S. citizens and adult children of legal permanent residents. The bills would make it virtually impossible for U.S. citizens to bring their parents here, by requiring purchase of health insurance and long term care insurance before the parent could immigrate; such insurance is both prohibitively expensive and difficult for many to obtain because of discrimination on the basis of age and ethnicity.

The Leadership Conference on Civil Rights is concerned that the proposed cuts in legal immigration appear to be aimed at the Latino and Asian American communities, and that some of the supporters of this approach base their arguments on explicitly racial grounds. The Leadership Conference opposes reductions in legal immigration which would punish these communities of Americans by making family reunification difficult or impossible, by directly cutting visas, or by such indirect means as increasing the earnings test for sponsorship of a family-based immigrant or requiring the purchase of health insurance. There is no credible evidence that family immigration presents social or economic problems for the U.S.; these initiatives not only harm Latino and Asian Americans, but also fly in the face of American family values.

Document G

2. Worker verification systems are of dubious merit

Both of the pending immigration bills call for the creation of pilot projects to test a national computer database of authorized workers, involving records from the Social Security Administration and the Immigration and Naturalization Service. Congress could act, upon conclusion of the pilot projects, to implement the verification system nationwide.

The employer sanctions experience indicates clearly that many employers respond to requirements to verify the work authorization of their workers in a way that fosters employment discrimination. According to the U.S. General Accounting Office, 19% of surveyed employers nationwide admitted that they engage in unlawful employment discrimination as a result of the employer sanctions law. Proponents assert that computer-based verification is a mechanism for both enhancing enforcement of employer sanctions and reducing discrimination, because the system would reduce employer confusion.

It is not clear, as proponents assert, that a computer verification system will reduce this discrimination. Experience does not support the assumption that employers will change their hiring practices as a result of a new high-tech verification scheme. Moreover, such a system is likely to engender new abuses of civil rights and liberties. The more Americans have access to an easy to use verification system, the more likely they are to use it in unauthorized ways: for example, to pre-screen "suspect" individuals before the hiring process, or to verify "foreign-looking" persons outside of the hiring context.

Once a system is created, policy makers will be tempted to authorize its use for a variety of other purposes, such as benefits eligibility, child care, law enforcement and health care, which is likely to increase undesired access to private information on working Americans, and to facilitate unwarranted invasions of privacy.

The Leadership Conference acknowledges that important procedural protections against discrimination, system errors, and unwarranted disclosures of sensitive information were added to the Senate bill, and recognizes that some have supported such protections out of concern about discrimination. Nevertheless, the Leadership Conference is unpersuaded that the institution of a national data base to verify the identity and employment of every newly-hired worker in the U.S. makes sense. Unless such a system can be implemented in a manner which will not engender further discrimination or endanger privacy rights, the Leadership Conference on Civil Rights will be obligated to oppose its enactment and implementation. Instead, our country should focus on raising labor standards and improving enforcement of existing standards, in order to reduce the attractiveness of undocumented workers to employers.

Source Citation: Leadership Conference on Civil Rights. "Statement on Pending Immigration Reform Statute." Reproduced in History Resource Center. Farmington Hills, MI: Gale Group.
http://galenet.galegroup.com/servlet/HistRC/
Document Number: CD2163000182

Proposition 187: Text of Proposed Law

This initiative measure is submitted to the people in accordance with the provisions of Article II, Section 8 of the Constitution.

This initiative measure adds sections to various codes; therefore, new provisions proposed to be added are printed in {+ italic type +} to indicate that they are new.

PROPOSED LAW

SECTION 1. Findings and Declaration.

The People of California find and declare as follows:

That they have suffered and are suffering economic hardship caused by the presence of illegal aliens in this state.

That they have suffered and are suffering personal injury and damage caused by the criminal conduct of illegal aliens in this state.

That they have a right to the protection of their government from any person or persons entering this country unlawfully.

Therefore, the People of California declare their intention to provide for cooperation between their agencies of state and local government with the federal government, and to establish a system of required notification by and between such agencies to prevent illegal aliens in the United States from receiving benefits or public services in the State of California.

SECTION 2. Manufacture, Distribution or Sale of False Citizenship or Resident Alien Documents: Crime and Punishment.

Section 113 is added to the Penal Code, to read:

{+ 113. Any person who manufactures, distributes or sells false documents to conceal the true citizenship or resident alien status of another person is guilty of a felony, and shall be punished by imprisonment in the state prison for five years or by a fine of seventy-five thousand dollars ($75,000). +}

SECTION 3. Use of False Citizenship or Resident Alien Documents: Crime and Punishment.

Section 114 is added to the Penal Code, to read:

{+ 114. Any person who uses false documents to conceal his or her true citizenship or resident alien status is guilty of felony, and shall be punished by imprisonment in the state prison for five years or by a fine of twenty-five thousand dollars ($25,000). +}

Source Citation: Unknown. "Proposition 187." Reproduced in History Resource Center. Farmington Hills, MI: Gale Group. http://galenet.galegroup.com/servlet/HistRC/
Document Number: CD2154000115

Notes